Wasted Youth

Raising achievement and tackling social exclusion

Nick Pearce and Josh Hillman

POLICY RESEARCH

INSTITUTE FOR PUBLIC POLICY RESEARCH

30-32 Southampton St
London WC2E 7RA
Tel: 020 7470 6100
Fax: 020 7470 6111
postmaster@ippr.org.uk
www.ippr.org.uk
Registered charity 800065

The Institute for Public Policy Research is an independent charity whose purpose is to contribute to public understanding of social, economic and political questions through research, discussion and publication. It was established in 1988 by leading figures in the academic, business and trade-union communities to provide an alternative to the free market think tanks.

IPPR's research agenda reflects the challenges facing Britain and Europe. Current programmes cover the areas of economic and industrial policy, Europe, governmental reform, human rights, defence, social policy, the environment and media issues.

Besides its programme of research and publication, IPPR also provides a forum for political and trade union leaders, academic experts and those from business, finance, government and the media, to meet and discuss issues of common concern.

Production & design by **EMPHASIS**
ISBN 1 86030 069 3
© IPPR 1998. Reprinted 1999 by Direct Image, London.

Contents

Preface

This publication is the result of a research project undertaken by IPPR between September 1997 and June 1998. It ranges across a broad policy terrain and as a result is deliberately synoptic, avoiding detailed prescription in any specific area. Many conclusions are provisional and have been put forward to stimulate further discussion and research.

The book focuses mainly on England and Wales, in terms of the statistics it draws on and in its references to institutional arrangements and qualifications structures. However, all of the issues raised and most of the policy prescriptions, will be of interest to the whole of the United Kingdom and perhaps beyond.

The authors would like to thank all those who have contributed to the ideas contained in this volume, through discussions, correspondence and at the seminar we held in December 1997. We would particularly like to thank the following, who gave us more than a fair share of time, energy and expertise: Liz Allen (The Education Network), David Bell (Newcastle City Council), Graham Badman (Oxfordshire County Council), Bob Coles (University of York), Prof. James Cornford (Cabinet Office), Lord Davies (Further Education Funding Council), Dan Finn (University of Portsmouth), Andy Green (University of London Institute of Education), Carol Hayden (University of Portsmouth), Robert Henderson (Strathmore Centre), Donald Hirsch, Ann Hodgson (University of London Institute of Education), Gerry Holtham (IPPR), Chris Humphries (TEC National Council), Philip Hunter (Staffordshire County Council), Ben Jamal (Richmond upon Thames Social Services), Reggie Kibel, Lindsay Mackie, Margaret Maden (Keele University), Jim McCormick (Scottish Council Foundation), Neil McIntosh (CFBT Education Services), Brian Merton (National Youth Agency), Peter Mitchell, Philip O'Hear (London Borough of Camden), Jim Pateman (Basic Skills Agency), Adrian Perry (Lambeth College), Peter Robinson (IPPR), Ruth Silver (Lewisham College), Sarah Spencer (IPPR), Ken Spours (University of London Institute of Education), Prof. Mike Thorne (Napier University), Lorna Unwin (University of Sheffield), Chris Webb (Cambridge Training and Development), Anne Weinstock (Rathbone CI), Alan Wells (Basic Skills Agency), Andrea Westall (IPPR) and Howard Williamson (University of Cardiff).

We are also grateful to Rathbone CI and Include for providing us with the opportunity to gain a first hand appreciation of their work. Last, but far from least, we would like to thank Anne Pinney of the University of London Institute for Education for the initial and invaluable literature review she undertook for the project. Naturally, none of the above carries any responsibility for the final version, which rests with the authors alone.

IPPR gratefully acknowledges financial support for this research project from CFBT Education Services.

Chapter 1: Education, disaffection and social exclusion

Introduction

Achievement in education fundamentally determines the course of an individual's life. The skills, knowledge and qualifications people acquire shape profoundly their participation in society. The prospects for those who leave school with little or nothing to show for it are poor. Many do not get a second chance. Yet a significant number of teenagers still do not participate in education or training, suffer low levels of achievement, or are in the current parlance 'disaffected' and 'socially excluded'.

The statistics paint a bleak picture:

- one in twelve young people leaves school without any qualifications;

- nearly one in three of those in their GCSE year does not get any passes at C or above;

- between 1991 and 1996 the annual number of permanent exclusions rose from 2,910 to 13,581;

- over 100,000 young people are excluded temporarily each year;

- nearly one in ten Year 11 pupils truants at least once a week;

- 7 per cent of 16 year olds and 8-9 per cent of 17 year olds are not in education, training or employment, with local studies showing much higher figures than these.

Whilst only very small numbers of young people suffer multiple deprivation, many individuals fall into several of these quantifiable categories. The statistical links between truancy, exclusion, non-participation and low attainment are well founded in the evidence. So are their links with criminal and other socially corrosive activities.

Focus for this report

This report focuses on two overlapping groups of young people:

- those who under-achieve, truant, drop-out or are excluded from compulsory education; and

- those who do not participate in education and training after leaving school.

Under-achievement, of course, extends well beyond these two groups. There are many young people who stay on in full-time education but have poor exam results and much larger numbers who stay in the system but are not nearly achieving their potential. Indeed, in the long term it is only through strategies that aim to raise achievement and participation amongst all young people, that the needs of the so-called 'excluded' can be addressed.

However, policy-making has been blighted by the tradition of considering 14-16 and 16-19 year olds in separation from each other, by neglect of issues around the key transition point at age 16, and by a tendency to be constrained by professional, institutional and organisational boundaries that prevent an integrated approach to individual needs. It is a chief contention of this report that selective or age-constrained policy frameworks have failed to raise achievement, at all levels. Our recommendations therefore concern the full range of learning provision for the 14-19 year old age group.

Although this volume touches on wider issues of public policy and practice, it does not seek to cover the broad canvas of youth issues. Nonetheless, we contend that effective strategies to raise educational achievements of all 14-19 year olds require policy co-ordination across established departmental and professional boundaries. We seek to indicate areas for further policy articulation wherever possible.

The seeds of disaffection

There is a widespread consensus that the seeds of disaffection and low attainment are sown well before secondary schooling and that early years education must have priority in the drive to raise standards. We have no doubt that strategies to tackle disaffection and under-achievement require a full range of effective policies from the very start of a child's education, and that the impact of these policies will be greater than those aimed at the secondary and tertiary phases. Consequently, the Government's policies for universal nursery provision, raising standards in primary schools, and tackling the serious problem of poor basic skills at Key Stage 2, are all very welcome.

In the best-case scenario, these policies will be implemented quickly and will be successful. But even in this scenario, there will be for some time – and perhaps always – a cohort of young people who reach the critical transition age of 14 at risk of under-achievement and disengagement from compulsory education, and another that leaves school at 16 and does not participate in any education and training. There is, however, not nearly enough evidence about the genesis of disaffection nor about the way that young people change during their teenage years. It is to this important period of later adolescence that this report is addressed.

In the rest of this chapter we focus explicitly on issues of disaffection, under-achievement and non-participation to put the more inclusive approach described into context.

Disaffected young people: a youth underclass?

The image of disaffected youth has become a familiar one in contemporary societies. Most commonly, it is one of sullen or aggressive, deviant and criminal young men, cut adrift from the norms and day-to-day life of the mainstream community. It is an image which occupies a powerful place in the social imagination. So dangerous and dislocated from the fabric of society do these young people appear that they are explicitly dehumanised in press reports and elsewhere: the young man becomes a 'ratboy', or 'spiderboy', one of a pack of feral 'underwolves'. Distorted portrayals of disaffection are not confined to male youths, as is shown by the stigmatisation of teenage single parents, particularly by the media.

It would be easy simply to dismiss these images as media constructs. But behind the headlines lies an important and often heated debate. Is there a new youth underclass – a subsection of a wider underclass – that is anti-social, criminal and feckless, and distinct from, and hostile to, wider society? Or is the notion of a youth underclass a populist, politically motivated and intellectually indefensible concept?

The underclass debate

It is generally recognised that there are at least four broad positions in the contemporary underclass debate (for example, see MacDonald in MacDonald ed., 1997). The first is that associated with Charles Murray and the Conservative Right, which posits the existence of a distinct stratum of society which has emerged to a large extent as a result of the predominance of liberal welfare policies and liberal values in contemporary capitalist societies. According to this view the underclass is composed of individuals who are morally irresponsible, parasitic upon wider society and corrosive of its normative foundations and social stability. It is the behaviour (and even the genetic makeup) of this section of society – expressed in such phenomena as long-term unemployment, single parenthood and criminal activity – which defines it as an underclass.

The second version accepts the emergence of an underclass but relocates causal responsibility in wider social structural phenomena. Economic and social change – particularly the decline of manual jobs in extractive and manufacturing industries – has destroyed the basis of traditional working class communities, large parts of which have been forced into long-term welfare dependency and social marginalisation. For many members of this non-working class, this structural exclusion from the material bases of community life generates adaptive behaviour, such as participation in the informal economy, use of hard drugs and criminal activity.

A third position is less committed. Its proponents recognise that profound economic, social and cultural changes have taken place in advanced capitalist societies, but they are as yet unconvinced that the empirical data supports the identification of a coherent and distinct underclass. They are prepared to accept the theoretical possibility of an underclass but not without further analysis and investigation.

In contrast, the fourth and final position rejects the concept of an underclass altogether. It considers the concept to have no theoretical validity or supporting foundation in empirical trends and regards the identification of an 'underclass' as simplistic and ideologically-motivated. In this view the concept serves to obscure disparate processes of social exclusion and, in so doing, supports the development of misinformed and potentially dangerous social policy.

These positions provide a frame of reference to analyses concerned with disaffected youth. Like those who regard the concept of an underclass as simplistic, we focus in this report on the specific social and institutional factors which generate or perpetuate exclusion from mainstream education and training participation for different groups of young people. Although this report is primarily concerned with education and training, we do not find supporting evidence for the existence or emergence of a distinct youth underclass.

Understanding disaffection

Choice and circumstance

While this report focuses heavily on the role of socio-economic and institutional structures and practices, we do not deny the importance of individual behavioural factors, including delinquent and criminal activity, in the discussion of disaffection. We are on familiar sociological ground here: these arguments rehearse debates regarding the respective roles and causal weight of structure and agency in the explanation of social phenomena. Crudely put, for example, disaffection can be viewed primarily as a manifestation of cultural or individual dispositions, the response to which should be behavioural sanctions or inducements. At the polar opposite, disaffection can be viewed largely as an effect of systemic or structural determinants, the fundamental amelioration or overhaul of which must be the primary object of policy intervention.

This report follows much social theory in rejecting the dualism of structure and agency. It recognises that social structures are the necessary condition of any intentional activity but also insists that these structures are reproduced and transformed through human agency. This has obvious consequences for the analysis of the education and training of young people, including those identified as disaffected or disengaged. It means we must take account of both the economic, social and institutional determinants of activity and circumstance, and the choices and agency of young people in response to the opportunity structures they confront, and the blocks in those structures. (Cloward and Ohlin, 1961; Coles, 1995).

In policy-making terms, all of this requires us to locate the 'problem' of disaffection simultaneously at a number of levels – socio-economic, institutional and individual – and to formulate our response accordingly.

Defining disaffection

For many commentators and practitioners, the very use of the term 'disaffection' is controversial because it implies that the behaviour and circumstances of some of the most disadvantaged young people in our society are primarily the result of their own individual attitudes and decisions. This is held to deflect attention from wider social and institutional determinants of educational participation and achievement, and encourage divisive policy solutions which are addressed to a selected group of young people. For this reason, many choose to refer instead to disengagement (which strictly speaking suffers from some of the same problems) or, more broadly, to social exclusion. Moreover, disaffection appears a difficult term to use because there is no commonly cited or widely accepted definition of it in official or academic literature. Disaffection is analysed and defined within a multiplicity of discursive contexts and this complicates its use as a descriptive or analytical tool.

In short, seeking to define a specific *category* of disaffected young people is likely to prove fruitless. However, it is clear that the term disaffection has broad currency and, for ease of reference, this report refers largely to 'disaffected' young people. This does not mean that we understand disaffection simply to be a behavioural problem or that our recommendations are of a selective or partial nature. Throughout the report our concern is with *inclusive* education and training strategies which raise levels of achievement for all young people. This means, as stated above, that we address ourselves in what follows not only to disaffected young people but more broadly to those who under-achieve or do not participate in 14-19 education and training. We are also aware that for some young people conventional notions of 'achievement' and 'participation' are an inadequate definition of success and self-esteem.

Although we follow the practice of broadly distinguishing disaffected or disengaged young people from those with special educational needs or emotional and behavioural difficulties, we recognise that this can only be a rule of thumb and, indeed, that labelling processes can often mask a failure to realise inclusivity in education. Furthermore, disaffection might be seen as a rational response to the circumstances of many young people. And whilst the media (and many researchers) tend to focus on the most visible manifestations of disaffection, in particular rebellious or criminal behaviour, it is important to note that most survey research on young people points to their conformist and conservative aspirations (DES, 1983; David, 1990; Industrial Society, 1997).

For the purposes of this report we examine disaffection on the basis of trends and issues in exclusion, non-attendance and under-achievement of pupils in compulsory education. For the 16-19 age group, we analyse the so-called 'Status Zero' group of those not participating in education, training or employment, and look at problems of low attainment across different post-16 pathways.

Non-participation and under-achievement

Why should we focus on under-achievement and non-participation? To begin with, studies have consistently shown that educational attainment at 16 is the most important predictor of future participation in learning and of labour market prospects. Yet at present, some 8 per cent of 16 year olds leave school without having obtained any GCSE passes at all, a proportion which has remained stubbornly constant in recent years despite rises in aggregate levels of achievement.

After completion of compulsory schooling, approximately 8 per cent of 16 year olds do not participate in education, training or employment. Although many will move in and out of this non-participant group as they get older, the scale of low attainment is such that by age 19, 30 per cent of young people have still not reached level 2 qualifications (notionally equivalent to 5 GCSEs at grade A* – C). Educational disadvantage stays with a large part of this group for life: 36 per cent of adults have done no education and training since leaving school, and a large proportion of these have no qualifications at all (Sargant and Tuckett, 1996).

This represents a long tail of low educational attainment in the United Kingdom which it shares with the United States but not with most of Continental Europe, where levels of participation and achievement in 14-19 education and training are higher. The UK falls below the OECD mean for net enrolment in full and part-time education for each of the 16, 17 and 18 year old age groups (OECD, 1997). As regards attainment, the UK, with the high levels of young people it has in the no or low skills category, stands in stark contrast to France and Germany. The attainment profile of 25-28 year olds in the UK, like that of the US, shows a 'hollowing out' of level 2 and 3 qualifications, so that the largest groups are those with no or low skills, and those with degrees (Green and Steedman, 1997).

As will be shown in the next two chapters, the issue is not simply one of the distribution of educational attainment. Other problems that will be examined include:

●   differences in achievement between boys and girls in compulsory education;

●   the steep rise in recent years in those excluded from school;

- different types of truanting and their impact on achievement and participation in post-compulsory education and training;

- the groups of young people most at risk of under-achievement, truancy, school exclusion and crime.

The political context

High levels of under-achievement and non-participation in education and training of 14-19 year olds – and the social consequences of this failure – have helped give renewed political prominence to issues of disaffection and disengagement. Of course, political attention to these issues is not new. From the late 1970s onwards the rise in youth unemployment began to undercut established school-to-work transitions, and meanwhile national crime statistics rose sharply. Since then, local authorities, central government and other agencies have pursued numerous initiatives aimed at under-achievers or those considered at risk of disengagement from mainstream education and training provision. Many of these initiatives have proved innovative and successful, but the majority of activity has remained piecemeal, resourced only for limited duration, with scarce resources dispersed across organisations and statutory bodies. There has been no real attempt by policy-makers to consolidate this activity.

With the publication of the Dearing Review of 16-19 qualifications in 1996, a selective focus on a group of young people identified as disaffected or under-achieving emerged at the level of national policy. The review's recommendations – for the development of new Entry level qualifications and co-ordinated national support for local partnership activities – were taken up and elaborated in the 1996 White Paper, *Learning to Compete,* self-proclaimed as the first document of its kind to address 14-19 education and training issues as a totality. Whether a Conservative government would have fully implemented its proposals is a moot point. It should be remembered that the philosophy of the paper was very much at odds with – and even stood in condemnation of – the rest of that government's strategy for the introduction of quasi-markets into tertiary education. This approach afforded limited attention to those who were, in whatever sense, 'excluded', and were as a result increasingly neglected by intense competition between providers to recruit learners.

In fact, many of the proposals contained in the White Paper have since been subsumed into wider policy programmes initiated by the Labour government. As a consequence of activity on a number of fronts, the political salience of the issue of disaffection and under-achievement in education has risen considerably. The Education and Employment Select Committee recently (1998) undertook a short inquiry on 'disaffected children'. It was explicitly, and particularly, concerned about the substantial extra public expenditure, both direct and indirect, associated with this group.

The Department for Education and Employment has now embarked upon a series of measures to raise levels of educational achievement amongst 14-19 year olds, including specific policies – in particular, the New Start strategy – addressed to disaffected and disengaged young people. Truancy and exclusions from school formed one of the first areas of inquiry of the new and potentially powerful Social Exclusion Unit (1998), whose far-reaching and important recommendations form part of the backdrop to this report. And with explicit reference to the critical role of education and training provision, the Home Office has legislated to draw together different agencies and authorities at a local level for greater co-ordination of action to tackle youth crime. These and other government initiatives will be examined in the following chapters.

Structure of the rest of the report

In Chapter Two, we look at key trends and issues in under-achievement, exclusions and truancy for the 14-16 year old age group. In Chapter Three, we examine the scope of the problem of non-participation and low achievement in education, training and employment in the 16-19 year old age group. In Chapter Four we look at current initiatives, including effective micro-strategies, for tackling disaffection and raising achievement within the existing system of 14-19 education and training, concluding with a brief discussion of more radical ways ahead.

In Chapter Five we look at the qualification and curricular structures of 14-19 education and training, particularly in respect of disaffected, disengaged and vulnerable groups. We examine options for the development of a more inclusive system. In Chapter Six we look at the organisational framework of tertiary provision and also discuss reform of services for disadvantaged young people. In each case we examine options for development in the medium and longer terms. In Chapter

Seven we look at how individuals and institutions are funded in the 14-19 phase of education and training. Finally, in Chapter Eight we draw together the themes of the report and summarise our policy recommendations.

Chapter 2: Under-achievement and disaffection in schools

In this chapter we examine the extent and nature of disaffection in schools. We look first at low attainment and under-achievement, before turning to key trends and issues in school exclusions and truancy. We then look at the school context in which disaffection occurs, including factors which are commonly identified as contributing to the disaffection of pupils at Key Stage 4.

Low attainment and under-achievement in compulsory education

There is a long tail of low attainment in compulsory education. Table 2.1 shows the extent of this tail. Although there have been year-on-year improvements in the proportion of young people achieving five GCSE A*-C grades since the late 1980s, the proportion of pupils leaving school without any GCSE passes has remained stubbornly constant at around 1 in 12, with three-quarters of these not having even been entered for examinations at all. As a result, the gap between those with the lowest levels of attainment and the rest of their peers is widening.

Table 2.1: GCSE/GNVQ attempts and achievements by 15 year old pupils (England, end 1996/7)

Year	No of 15 year old pupils	% entered for 5+ GCSEs or equivalent	% gained 5+ A*-C grades or equivalent	% gained 5+ A*-G grades or equivalent	% entered for 1+ GCSEs or equivalent	% gained 1+ A*-C grades or equivalent	% gained A*-G grades or equivalent
1996/7	586,682	89.6	45.1	86.4	94.0	70.5	92.3
1995/6	594,035	89.3	44.5	86.1	93.9	70.2	92.2
1994/5	578,197	89.3	43.5	85.7	93.8	69.2	91.9
1993/4	532,273	89.1	43.3	85.6	94.2	69.7	92.3

Source: DfEE Statistical Press Notice 386/97

There is a common perception that there is an achievement gap between boys and girls in compulsory education, with girls outperforming boys in both National Curriculum assessments and at GCSE. In fact, at the lowest levels of attainment, gender performance differences are not that great. Overall the proportion of 15 year olds not achieving passes in the core subjects of the National Curriculum (English, maths and science) has fallen in recent years but as Table 2.2 shows, 15 per cent of girls still leave school without securing a GCSE pass in each of the core subjects, as compared to 19 per cent of boys. There is a marked gender gap in English but otherwise there are almost as many girls at the lowest level of attainment as boys.

These figures suggest that policies for tackling under-achievement should not be driven by stereotypes of disaffection which portray only boys as failing or being failed. Indeed they present a strong case for policy-makers and practitioners better to address the needs of under-achieving girls at Key Stage 4.

Table 2.2: GCSE/GNVQ attempts and achievements by 15 year old pupils (England, end 1996/7)

	No of 15 year old pupils	% not entered for any GCSEs	% not gaining any GCSEs	% not achieving a GCSEs pass in English	% not achieving a GCSEs pass in in Maths	% not achieving a GCSEs pass in in English and Maths	% not achieving a pass in English, Maths and Science
Boys	299,475	6.9	8.8	13	14	17	19
Girls	287,207	5.0	6.5	9	12	13	15

Source: adapted from DfEE Statistical Press Notice 386/97

In fact, the gender gap is much wider at higher grades: 50 per cent of girls achieved at least 5 A*-C grades or the GNVQ equivalent in 1996/7, compared to 40 per cent of boys. It is particularly marked in English: 59 per cent of girls achieved grade A*-C in English GCSE in 1996/7, compared to 41 per cent of boys. As in so many aspects of education, the experience at the top end of the system has an undue effect on both policy-making and the media.

Although data on the achievements of different ethnic minorities are not collected nationally, research indicates certain observable patterns (Gillborn & Gipps, 1996 quoted in Tomlinson ed. 1997). Inequalities in educational achievement persist for some ethnic groups, despite general improvements in attainment. Afro-Caribbean boys are particularly vulnerable to low achievement but Afro-Caribbean girls also experience inequality in achievement levels. According to the Youth Cohort Study, under a quarter of Afro-Caribbean young people reached 5 or more A*-C GCSEs in 1996. Young people from Indian backgrounds appear to perform consistently better than other South Asians, and achieve average results which are higher than their white peers in some areas. Bangladeshis and Pakistanis do less well and are over-represented in ungraded groups (Gillborn in Tomlinson ed., 1997).

Particular groups of young people – often overlapping – have significantly low levels of educational attainment, such as those in care and young offenders. Surveys have suggested that three-quarters of those who have been looked after by local authorities have no qualifications when they leave school and that only one or two in every hundred will achieve an A level pass (Garnett, 1992: 63). These young people are overwhelmingly from low income backgrounds and bring significant educational disadvantage with them into care. However, rather than ameliorate this disadvantage, the experience of care appears to compound it (Biehal *et al*, 1995: 58), which stands as a serious indictment of policy in this area.

Low attainment or under-achievement in schools is not, of course, a direct indicator of disaffection, although it may partially reflect disenchantment with learning. Partnerships between local agencies to tackle disaffection commonly rely on more tangible indicators of disaffection, such as exclusion and truancy, to inform their strategies.

School exclusions

That the issue of disaffection must be analysed at a number of levels – socio-economic, institutional and individual – is made strikingly clear in relation to school exclusion. Exclusion is the ultimate sanction a school may employ against a pupil who is persistently disobedient, disruptive, or violent.[1] Excluded pupils, or those at risk of exclusion, form a core of those young people at whom strategies to tackle disaffection are directed. But exclusion cannot be explained merely as a response to disaffected behaviour, however extreme that behaviour may be. Analysis of exclusion statistics shows that institutional factors must be given as much consideration as the background and behaviour of individuals in explaining the incidence of exclusion. Indeed, the very act of exclusion is in most cases directed towards the needs of the school rather than those of the individual being dealt with. Furthermore, justification for exclusion is not based on well-established criteria: DfEE guidance is vague and until now has not been enforced by statute.

The growth in exclusions

Official figures show that there were 12,500 permanent exclusions from primary, secondary and special schools in 1995/6, an increase of 13 per cent in relation to the previous year (DfEE, 1997a). Survey evidence suggests that the level could be even higher and as Table 2.3 (Parsons/DfEE, 1995) shows, the number has risen considerably year-on-year since the implementation of the 1988 Education Reform Act, although the most recent figures indicate that this rise may have reached a plateau (Godfrey & Parsons, 1998). As the Social Exclusion Unit points out, these figures only cover exclusions in any given year, and do not include young people excluded in a previous year and still out of school, nor those excluded 'informally' (Social Exclusion Unit, 1998).

In addition to these permanent exclusions, fixed term exclusions are estimated to run at about eight times the level of permanent exclusions with around 100,000 from secondary schools a year (exclusions not pupils), although figures for trends are not available (OFSTED, 1996). Pupils in England and Wales are now losing more than half a million school days each year as a result of being temporarily excluded or suspended from school (Smith, 1998).

Table 2.3 Permanent exclusions from schools in England

Year	Number of permanent exclusions
1990/1	2,910
1991/2	3,833
1992/3	8,636
1993/4	11,181
1994/5	12,458
1995/6	13,581
1996/7	13,453

Source: Parsons/DfEE 1995, Parsons 1996, Godfrey & Parsons, 1998

The rise in exclusions cannot be attributed to a sudden surge in disruptive behaviour, or to underlying socio-economic change. Institutional factors appear to have been the major cause. These include:

- the specific performance indicators – league tables – to which schools have been subject, which provide a disincentive to concentrate resources or effort on those least likely to achieve (or, conversely, more likely to disrupt the education of other pupils);

- funding disincentives to educate difficult pupils in the mainstream. Only as a consequence of the Education Act 1993 was provision made to ensure that funding follows an excluded pupil out of the school setting – until the 1994/5 academic year, schools therefore had a direct resource incentive to exclude difficult pupils. Moreover, only now, as a consequence of the Social Exclusion Unit's report, will they have a resource incentive to include these pupils;

- institutional divisions between schools, particularly the independence of grant-maintained schools from local authorities, which allowed them greater selectivity over the admission of previously excluded pupils;

- the constraints imposed by the National Curriculum crowding the timetable and limiting the scope of teachers to address the needs of pupils who may be struggling;

- the previous set of National Targets for Education and Training, which ignored the lowest achievers;

- lower tolerance levels amongst teachers, partly due to the policy positions of certain teacher associations.

Who is being excluded?

The fact that specific groups of young people are more vulnerable to exclusion than others has long been recognised. In practice, however, the problem has not been adequately addressed.[2] The majority of permanent exclusions – 83 per cent in 1995/6 – are from secondary schools, although there has also been a clear upward trend in primary exclusions which have now reached disturbingly high levels and which require a different policy approach (Hayden, 1997).

The number of exclusions rises sharply when pupils reach age thirteen and peaks at age fourteen. Together, fourteen and fifteen year olds account for nearly half of all permanent exclusions (DfEE, 1997a). Consequently, Key Stage 4 is a critical phase for alternative provision to allow transfer of those about to be excluded, and preventative intervention strategies need to come in the earlier years of secondary school.

Clear groups of young people are at disproportionate risk of exclusion:

- *Boys*

  The overwhelming majority of those permanently excluded – 83 per cent – are boys. The gender difference is greatest in primary schools but still extensive, at a ratio of four to one, in secondary exclusions (Parsons, 1996; OFSTED, 1996).

- *Afro-Caribbean pupils*

  Afro-Caribbean and other black pupils suffer disproportionately high rates of permanent exclusion. The overall percentage of the compulsory school population permanently excluded in 1995/6 was 0.19 per cent, but for Afro-Caribbean pupils the percentage was significantly higher at 0.92 per cent (DfEE, 1997a). There is little or no evidence as to what lies behind these figures.

- *Young people from lower socio-economic groups*

  OFSTED has found some correlation between the socio-economic context of the school and its exclusion rate, using free school meals as an indicator (OFSTED, 1996). However, it has also noted that some schools with a high level of disadvantage do maintain a very low rate of exclusion, and vice versa. Other research has indicated that young people from poorer families are more likely to be excluded than their peers (Hayden, 1997).

- *Young people with disturbed or disrupted family circumstances*

  Many of those excluded from school have disturbed or disrupted home contexts: family break-up through divorce or separation, bereavement, chronic illness, alcoholism, violence and abuse (Hayden, 1997; OFSTED, 1996).

● *Looked-after young people*

Young people who are looked after by local authorities are one of the groups most at risk of exclusion. The joint OFSTED/Social Services Inspectorate (1995) report found that 12 per cent of those of school age in care were either excluded or did not attend school on a regular basis, rising to 26 per cent for 14 – 16 year olds. These are startling figures which are related to the problems of underachievement discussed earlier in the chapter, and they represent severe disadvantage for the group in negotiating complex transitions – entry into the labour market and securing accommodation and independence – in their late teens. Many do not do so successfully and simply exchange care placements for custodial sentences: nearly 40 per cent of the under-21s in prisons have been in care.

● *Young people with special educational needs*

The incidence of exclusion amongst those with special education needs or emotional and behavioural difficulties is around six times higher than for others (DfEE, 1997a). In many cases the act of exclusion triggers the statementing process (indeed, the exclusion process may be pursued deliberately by a school in order to secure faster access to additional resources for a young person). However, the exclusion of a young person on the grounds of special needs or emotional and behavioural difficulties may represent a response to disciplinary problems or the perceived costs of educating a pupil within a mainstream environment. There is a large overlap between the categories of pupils excluded for disruptive behaviour and those categorised as having special needs or emotional and behavioural difficulties (Booth in Blyth and Milner, eds., 1996), and the number of pupils formally identified as having emotional and behavioural needs is increasing (Farrell & Mittler, 1998).

School and LEA effects

There are also clearly observable school and LEA effects in patterns of exclusion. Inspection reports and academic studies have recorded strong differences in the propensity of schools to exclude young people. The 1996 OFSTED report on secondary school exclusions argued that:

schools' practice with regard to exclusions varied to an unacceptable degree. Some schools were far to ready too exclude; others did so with extreme reluctance. (OFSTED, 1996: 7).

The same conclusion had been reached in 1992 by the then Department for Education, which noted that variations in exclusion rates between schools were too great to be explained by socio-economic catchment area (DfEE, 1992). A recent study found that a quarter of secondary schools account for 65 per cent of permanent exclusions, and that half of secondary schools exclude only one or no pupils (Donovan, 1998). Indeed, school factors may be a more significant predictor of pupil exclusion than the actual behaviour of pupils (Imich, 1994). Anecdotal evidence, often reported in the press, suggests that many schools exclude pupils for the most minor transgressions.

At local authority level, Parsons' 1995 survey revealed that rates of permanent exclusion in some LEAs were ten times higher than in others. Once again, the variation was much higher than could be explained by the socio-economic characteristics of the area, suggesting a clear local authority influence.

The fact that certain groups of young people are at greater risk of exclusion than others, and that exclusion rates vary considerably between schools and local authorities, is recognised by central government, and has been at least since the early 1990s. The Labour government's first White Paper, *Excellence in Schools,* stated that the present rate of exclusions is 'too high' and raised particular concern over the 'unjustified variation in exclusion rates between schools and the disproportionate exclusion of pupils from certain ethnic minorities and young people looked after by local authorities.' (DfEE, 1997g: 57). The Social Exclusion Unit has said the same.

Provision for excluded young people

The importance of addressing the issues raised above cannot be overestimated, since the educational consequences of exclusion for the young people involved are extremely serious. Of those who are permanently excluded, few will be successfully reintegrated: only 27 per cent of primary age pupils and 15 per cent of secondary pupils return to mainstream schooling (Parsons/DfEE, 1995). Table 2.4 shows the breakdown for secondary pupils. Prospects for those excluded in Year

10 or Year 11 are particularly poor. The majority enter what Sir Ron Dearing called the 'educational limbo' of home tuition or a Pupil Referral Unit (PRU). Such out-of-school education is overwhelmingly part-time. The average number of hours per week of home tuition may be as little as five hours (Parsons/DfEE, 1995).

There are also serious concerns about the cost and the quality of provision for young people who do not return to mainstream school. It has been estimated that alternative provision costs around four times more, but that young people receive on average 10 per cent of actual education (Parsons, 1996). Inspection reports (OFSTED, 1993, 1995b) have been heavily critical of the provision made for excluded pupils in out-of-school PRUs. Inspectors have drawn attention to low expectations, confused objectives and low standards:

Table 2.4 Provision for excluded secondary pupils

Type of provision	% of excluded pupils
Return to mainstream school	15
Pupil Referral Unit	39
Home tuition	27
FE provision	8
Other (including none)	11

Source: Parsons/DfEE, 1995

---

in most units the education lacked a clear purpose... intellectual stimulus was weak and the work was well below pupils' age and ability (OFSTED, 1993: 5); and

overall the quality of teaching in the PRUs inspected fell below that found generally in mainstream primary and secondary schools and well below the quality necessary to gain the improvements in attainment required for successful reintegration into schools. (OFSTED, 1995b: 5)

In addition to problems of quality and standards, there are also concerns that PRUs engender peer-group effects in a similar fashion to the much-discussed consequences of being in prison. According to this view, young people in PRUs often develop or re-inforce identities and attitudes which confirm their sense of exclusion and of alienation from mainstream society. Instead of re-inforcing the identity of these young people as 'disaffected', they should be enabled to benefit from a greater mix of role models.

Where PRUs work well they can have a dramatic effect on attendance, motivation and achievement. There are plenty of lessons that can be learned from examining good practice. In particular, small pupil-centred units focused on the core and personal curriculum have been shown to enable reasonable success at GCSE for many young people excluded at Key Stage 4. Another often successful model has been where units are located within schools, offering alternative provision prior to exclusion.

However, as the Education and Employment Select Committee argues, PRUs 'should be not be seen as a permanent solution, but as one stage in the process of tackling exclusion'. The Committee also suggests that the Government should take action to attract higher quality staff and to put a higher quality curriculum in place in PRUs.

Truancy

In a sense, truancy is a voluntary form of exclusion on the part of the young person. Frequent truanting is the clearest expression of disaffection with school and dissatisfaction with the education provided. Evidence as to the precise reasons why pupils abscond from lessons is limited. Table 2.5 shows the results of one survey.It is likely that these figures over-estimate factors relating to the education provided by schools and under-estimate:

- peer-group pressures;

- families condoning their children taking time out of schools to work or share domestic responsibilities;

- instability caused by frequent change of school;

- bullying specifically, which other surveys show to affect attendance to a much greater extent.

Table 2.5: Causes of Truancy

Reasons given by pupils for truanting	% of excluded pupils
Irrelevant lessons	24
Dislike of teacher	19
Dislike of subject	15
Coursework problems	13
Difficulty of subject	9
Poor teaching	2
Bullying	1

Source: O'Keefe (1994)

The extent of truancy

Reliable and comprehensive information on the extent of truancy is difficult to assemble. Information on unauthorised absence from school (or truancy and absence that is condoned by parents but unjustified) is collected each year by the Department for Education and Employment and published in the secondary school performance tables and the accompanying national pupil absence tables (see Table 2.6). However, these figures underestimate levels of truancy, principally because they do not take account of the most common form of truancy: pupils who turn up for registration but fail to attend lessons. Nor do they take account of those pupils whose absence from school is not only condoned by parents but also by the schools, including cases where the school unofficially removes the pupil from the school roll.

Table 2.6: Unauthorised absence from maintained (LEA and GM) secondary schools in England

Indicator	School Year				
	1992/3	1993/4	1994/5	1995/6	1996/7
Percentage of half days missed	1.0	0.9	1.0	1.0	1.0
Average number of half days missed per absent pupil	24	22	22	21	20

Source: DfEE National Pupil Absence Tables 1993-7

More detailed material is provided by the report, Truancy in English Secondary Schools (O'Keefe, 1994), based on a questionnaire completed by 37,000 pupils in Years 10 and 11 in 1992. This report also underestimates the extent of truancy (as the questionnaire was only completed by pupils attending school on a particular day!) but nonetheless provides useful material on the frequency of truanting (see Table 2.7). The results of the survey show that nearly 10 per cent of pupils truant at least once a week or more and 5.4 per cent truant twice a week or more in the final year of compulsory education. There is a steep rise in the prevalence of truancy between Years 10 and 11, particularly amongst boys.

Table 2.7: Frequency of truancy in years 10 and 11 in England

	% of all pupils	% of Year 10 pupils	% of Year 11 pupils
Every day	1.5	1.3	1.6
2-4 times a week	3.2	2.6	3.8
Once a week	3.5	2.5	4.5
2-3 times a month	5.4	4.0	6.8
Once a month	4.7	4.0	5.5
Less often	12.2	10.8	13.6
Never	69.5	74.8	64.2

Source: O'Keefe (1994)

These findings are broadly congruent with those of the Youth Cohort Study (YCS). The YCS collects data from a sample of the cohort in England and Wales in the Spring following the completion of compulsory education, and therefore cannot provide definitive evidence on the extent of truancy. Nor can we directly compare YCS data with the results of the O'Keefe survey, as the frequencies used for categorising patterns of truancy are different. However, the YCS does allow us to examine changes in the extent of truancy in Year 11 over a ten year period (see Table 2.8). The table shows that 4 per cent reported truanting persistently (either for several days at a time or for weeks at a time). The equivalent figure for Year 10 has been estimated at 2.6 per cent (Education and Employment Select Committee, 1998).

Interestingly, the YCS data shows that the percentage of the cohort reporting persistent truancy in Year 11 actually fell over the last ten years, whilst the percentage of those who report never having truanted has increased from 46 per cent to 60 per cent (DfEE, 1997b: 15). Based on these figures – which are likely to underestimate the problem – there would have been a hard core of persistent truants numbering between

23,000 – 28,000 out of a total school population (excluding special schools) of 565,000 15 year olds in England in 1994/5.

Table 2.8: Extent of truancy reported in Year 11

% of 16 year olds playing truant	1984/85	1987/88	1989/90	1990/91	1992/93	1994/95
For weeks at a time	3	2	3	2	2	2
For several days at a time	4	3	3	3	2	2
For particular days or lessons	10	10	10	8	7	7
For the odd day or lesson	35	35	37	36	32	28
Never	46	49	46	51	56	60
No answer	1	1	1	1	1	1

Source: DfEE evidence to Education and Employment Select Committee

Who is truanting?

The YCS provides material on the social and parental background of truants. The analysis of data from the cohort (YCS Cohort 5) which reached school leaving age in 1990 by Casey and Smith (1995) showed that truancy rates were higher for those whose parents were in lower social-economic groups, were unemployed, or who lived in social housing. The strongest correlation, however, was between truanting and parental circumstances: only 14 per cent of those living with both parents truanted, compared to 25 per cent of those living with only one parent, and 38 per cent of those living with neither parent.

Other indicators of higher rates of truancy are: prior educational attainment or literacy level (OFSTED, 1995); school attended (there is a statistically significant difference in the likelihood of truancy according to the particular school); and employment (young people who work part-time tend to truant more). This last factor is clearly an important one: many young people work illegally, but often with the collusion of their parents, in order to help maintain family incomes. Others may truant in order to undertake domestic caring responsibilities which allow other family members to work. The evidence does not show, however, that gender or ethnicity are significant indicators of propensity to truant.

Truancy, participation and achievement

Unlike other data sources, the YCS also allows us to gain an understanding of the correlation, if not causal relationship, between truanting and educational participation and achievement. Those who truant persistently achieve far less than their peers at school and are heavily represented in the numbers who do not participate in education and training after the end of compulsory education. The YCS suggests that while persistent truants are a small percentage of the age cohort, they form nearly one in five of 16 year old non-participants and nearly a quarter of those not in education, training or employment. Unsurprisingly, it also shows that the educational attainment of persistent truants is significantly lower than their peers: some 38 per cent of persistent truants reported that they had not attained any GCSEs in Year 11, compared with 3 per cent of non-truants.

However, persistent truancy does not inevitably lead to non-participation after compulsory education: 25 per cent of persistent truants reported participation in full-time education at 16 in Spring 1996 and a further 16 per cent participation in government supported training (DfEE, 1997b: 21-3). There is consequently clear scope for intervention to attract persistent truants back into education and training, and a need for a greater understanding of how this can be achieved.

Truancy, exclusion and youth offending

The connections between exclusion, truancy and youth offending are well documented. Policy-making has for some time been guided by the danger of the development of a 'criminal cycle' leading from the school gates to penal custody. Related to this, the fact that girls are much less likely to commit crimes has meant that policy-makers and the media have tended to focus more on truancy and exclusion amongst boys.

The Audit Commission study, *Misspent Youth* (Audit Commission, 1996) noted that 65 per cent of school-age offenders sentenced in court were persistent truants or had been excluded from school. Similarly, Home Office research has found a strong correlation between non-attachment to school and offending. In a study of self-reported offending amongst 14-25 year olds in England and Wales, researchers found that the odds of offending of those who truanted from school were almost three times higher than those who did not truant. A strong relationship between exclusion and offending was also shown (Graham & Bowling, 1995).

However, attempting to determine causal relationships between truancy, exclusion and offending is problematic. Exclusion may be a contributory cause of offending, given that the probability of delinquent behaviour is far higher for those who are excluded, but also a consequence of criminal behaviour. Similarly, although a young person who truants persistently may be exposed to a greater likelihood of involvement in delinquent behaviour, truanting is itself a form of behaviour that must be explained, and not simply causally related to offending.

In fact, truancy, like offending, is strongly related to low levels of parental supervision and poor parental relationships. Overall, the Home Office research found that:

> Taking both family and school factors together, parental supervision and truancy from school emerged as the two strongest correlates of starting to offend. Furthermore, parental supervision was also found to be a strong predictor of truancy. Thus those teenagers who spend considerable periods unsupervised by either parents or the school are more likely to engage in truancy and criminal activity than those who are not. However, a low level of parental supervision was found to be strongly related to getting on badly with one or both parents, which in turn was found to be more likely in single parent and step families. (Graham & Bowling, 1995: 49)

These conclusions reinforce the findings of the YCS data and have important consequences for policy, namely, that the role of parents (including local authorities as corporate parents) is critical to the prevention and reduction of exclusion and truancy, as well as youth offending. We explore these issues in Chapter 4.

Disaffection in the school context

As we have seen, different components of social and family background are strongly correlated with individual manifestations of disaffection. Meanwhile, specific institutional forces have been behind the steep rise in school exclusions in recent years. But in addition, there are particular features of mainstream education, particularly at Key Stage 4, and the way that young people relate to schools as institutions, which appear to contribute to the extent of disaffection and under-achievement in learning.

The National Curriculum

The National Curriculum is often cited, particularly by teachers, as a significant contributor to pupil disaffection. Of course, the idea that an academic curriculum fails to motivate significant numbers of pupils is far from new. Proponents of selection have long argued that different pupils should be offered different curricula, that different learning styles should be encouraged, and in particular that vocational study should be the norm for low achievers. But the identification of the National Curriculum as a factor constraining the capacity of teachers to engage pupils is a more specific and obviously recent complaint.

Three key themes emerge from the literature in respect of the impact of the national curriculum on disaffected pupils. First, it is suggested that the rigidity of the National Curriculum and assessment imperatives at Key Stage 4 exacerbate disaffection and demotivation. Teachers identify the content and delivery of the curriculum as too prescribed. It has limited their scope for planning learning to meet identified student needs, and it has reduced the expectations that they can make academic and vocational learning accessible to *all* students.

Whilst we would in no way advocate producing a non-academic curriculum for less academically able pupils, it is important to recognise that the National Curriculum has contributed to the 'disenfranchisement' of these pupils. Research surveys of pupil views (Kinder *et al*, 1996a) on disaffection identify the curriculum as the third most important cause of truancy and disruptive behaviour. Pupils view the curriculum as lacking relevance, stimulus and variety. Boredom features prominently in pupils' replies, although, as the researchers point out, this may simply mask pupil learning difficulties.

This points to the second complaint addressed at the National Curriculum, namely that reduced emphasis on basic literacy and numeracy at Key Stages 1 and 2 – prior to recent reforms – has contributed to disaffection in later years, as students lack the basic skills to cope with the demands of the curriculum. Literacy and numeracy skills are of course highly correlated with examination performance (Ekinsmith & Bynner, 1994) and poor language skills have been highlighted as a source of disaffection amongst young males in particular (Wragg, 1997). More widely, it is imperative to recognise that disaffection at Key Stage 4 often has its roots in low standards and inadequate support at earlier stages in a young person's education, and also the difficulty of transition from primary to secondary education (Keys & Fernandes, 1993).

Third, the National Curriculum leaves insufficient time for personal and social education and education for citizenship. As the Education and Employment Select Committee argues, where these elements are associated with clearly defined outcomes they can play a major role in re-engaging disaffected young people. Teacher surveys also report that staff identify the reduction in non-teaching and pastoral time consequent to the introduction of the National Curriculum as a key factor behind the problem of pupil disaffection (Kinder *et al*, 1996). This is congruent with OFSTED's finding that a key factor in reducing exclusions is the availability of appropriate pastoral support (OFSTED, 1996).

School performance tables

The academic orientation of the content and delivery of Key Stage 4 is reinforced by school performance tables. Media coverage of the tables focuses very heavily on the proportion of pupils obtaining five or more A*-C grades at GCSE. Schools thus have a major incentive to concentrate attention and resources on those pupils at the borderline of this category at the expense of under-achievers. The Government is currently working on the idea of having an additional average point score (including GNVQ points) and trying to develop tables that take into account the 'value added' by schools through pupil progress. The Education and Employment Select Committee has also recommended that the incentives for schools to withdraw under-achieving pupils from examinations be removed by including in the performance tables the number and proportion of pupils leaving without sitting exams.

Pupil-teacher relationships

The quality of the pupil-teacher relationship is central to the determination and mediation of disaffection. Kinder *et al* (1996a) found that the relationship with teachers was the second most important causal factor identified by pupils themselves in seeking to explain their disruptive behaviour, and that parents were also aware of the importance of this relationship (Kinder & Wilkin, 1998). Having low expectations of pupils, treating them with a 'lack of respect' or unfairly, led them to behave badly, as did poor self-presentation. Similarly,

OFSTED's inspection of education for disaffected pupils found that 'pupil behaviour was directly related to the quality of their relationship with individual teachers' (OFSTED, 1993: 1).

There is also an observable teacher effect on truancy levels (Casey & Smith, 1995). The likelihood of truancy appears reduced in schools in which a high proportion of teachers are trained graduates and there are low pupil-teacher ratios and low rates of staff turnover. Evidently, such factors may affect the quality of the pupil-teacher relationship, as trained graduates are likely to be younger, and smaller classes and staff continuity are likely to facilitate positive pupil-teacher relationships. Initial teacher training pays very little attention to strategies for dealing with behavioural problems, concentrating as it does almost exclusively on developing subject-specific skills. Likewise, initiatives for tackling disaffection work best when integrated with in-service training and professional development (Kinder & Wilkin, 1998).

Discipline

Effective discipline in schools is a critical factor in both the explanation and management of pupil disaffection. Failure to achieve an ordered environment in a school or classroom contributes to the process of pupil disaffection, which may then result in disruptive or violent behaviour and exclusion, with a clear negative impact on levels of achievement (Sammons *et al*, 1995). Furthermore, some pupils may become disaffected because of verbal and physical intimidation or abuse from their peers. Bullying and racism are major causes of non-attendance and disruptive behaviour (DES, 1989; Kinder *et al*, 1996, 1996a; OFSTED, 1993)[3].

Conclusion

From this overview of the extent and consequences of disaffection and under-achievement we can see that there are significant numbers of young people for whom compulsory education is failing badly. Under-achievement and school exclusion are particularly prevalent amongst young male Afro-Caribbeans and those in care. Boys in general are far more likely to be excluded from school, but girls are just as likely to truant and gender differences amongst the very lowest attainers are small. Overall, there is a long tail of low attainment in our schools which does significant damage to the labour market prospects and social well-being of the pupils concerned.

Observable patterns of disaffection can be traced to institutional determinants as much as to individual background and behaviour. This is particularly true in relation to exclusion, which government policy acknowledges to vary to unjustified degrees between different ethnic minorities and also between schools and between local authorities. We further explore some of these institutional issues in Chapter 4 and examine how strategies at the local level are attempting to break through the cycles of under-achievement and disaffection that national policies are unable to address. Firstly, however, we examine non-participation of 16-19 year olds in education, training and work.

Chapter 3: Non-participation & under-achievement amongst 16-19 year olds

In this chapter we examine 16-19 year olds who under-achieve in education, or who do not participate in education and training or in the labour market. The characteristics of non-participants are outlined, and the relationship between education participation and the labour market is discussed.

Participation in education and employment

Since the late 1980s, patterns of school-leavers' participation in education and employment have changed dramatically. The proportion staying on in full-time education has risen considerably, whilst that entering employment has declined. Fewer than half of all 16 year olds stayed on in full-time education in 1986; by the end of 1996, some 70 per cent did so (see Table 3.1). Conversely, today only one in ten of those leaving school goes directly into the regular labour market, compared to nearly half of the age group in 1979. Clearly, this rise in levels of participation is a change of enormous significance. The evidence suggests, however, that it may have peaked now, and indeed there has been a small but noticeable decline in the percentage of 16 year olds entering full-time education.

Table 3.1: Participation in education and training of 16-18 year olds, end 1996 (England)

Age	% in education	full-time education or training	government supported training	employer funded training	other education or training
16	**86.4**	70.3	9.3	2.0	4.8
17	**78.7**	58.0	10.6	3.3	6.7
18	**59.7**	38.1	8.1	4.5	9.0

Source: Adapted from Participation in Education and Training by 16-18 year olds in England, DfEE 159/1997

Attainment and achievement

Participation statistics mask high levels of non-completion and often low levels of attainment in different post-school routes. Of course, young people can derive benefits from participation in education without acquiring a qualification or completing a course. However, it is a matter of concern that in full-time education, some 30 per cent of students who embark on post-16 courses fail successfully to complete them and less than half progress from intermediate to advanced level (Green & Steedman, 1996). This is not a new problem: the influential 1993 Audit Commission/OFSTED report, *Unfinished Business*, estimated that over 150,000 young people were leaving full-time courses without achieving their end objective, at a cost to the public purse of some £500 million.[4] Serious problems of retention and under-achievement mean that improved levels of participation in full-time education of 16 year olds have not been matched by expected increases in qualifications attainment of 17 and 18 year olds. Moreover, as with non-participation, under-achievement at 16 tends to persist throughout the teenage years of individuals, and indeed throughout their lives.

Government-supported training has also failed adequately to equip young people with qualifications. Whilst the introduction of Modern Apprenticeships has helped to raise standards for those in work-based learning, the track record of government schemes is poor. Designed initially to fulfil a social rescue function and provide a bridge into the world of work, Youth Training (now being replaced by National Traineeships) and its numerous antecedents have routinely performed badly in levels of completion and attainment. The proportion of leavers gaining a full or part qualification was 55 per cent in the period September 1996 to August 1997 (DfEE, 1998a).[5] The rest had no formal qualifications to show for their efforts.

Prospects of educational progress for those school-leavers who enter the regular labour market are also low. Whilst more than two-thirds of those who obtain and complete apprenticeships (not just Modern Apprenticeships but in general) can expect to achieve a qualification, only a fifth of those who enter full-time work after leaving school attain any additional qualification (Payne, 1995b). Only a half of 16 and 17 year olds in regular employment receive structured off-the-job training (Robinson, 1998).

The extent of non-participation

'Status Zero'
Although the vast majority of 16-18 year olds are in some form of education and training, there is a proportion of young people which is

neither employed nor undertaking any formal education or training activity. This non-participation has exercised youth policy analysts considerably in the last decade and has been contentiously termed 'Status Zero' in intensive local analyses.[6] The concept of a status has been preferred by analysts to that of a group: these young people are not homogeneous and tend furthermore to move in and out of the non-participating category.

National figures

In broad terms the numbers of those not participating in education, training or employment (see Table 3.2) have fluctuated with the economic cycle, with the availability of government sponsored training places, and with demographic changes. They were at their highest in the early 1980s with nearly one in eight of 16 year olds not in education, training or employment. This was a time in which a bulge in the youth cohort coincided with a recession. The 'excluded' group fell substantially in the late 1980s, before rising again in the early 1990s. But the rise in the 1990s was relatively slight, since this time the recession was less severe, and it coincided with a demographic downturn.

Table 3.2: Non-participation in education and training of 16-18 year olds by economic activity and age, end 1996 (England, '000s)

	16-18	16	17	18
Total in age group 16-18	1,780	619	604	557
Not in education or training	437	84	129	224
In employment	276	42	78	155
ILO unemployed	91	29	23	39
Economically inactive	71	13	27	31

Source: School, college and trainee records, Labour Force Survey

The number of young people not in education, training or employment is a matter of debate. In estimating the number of non-participants across the country, we have to compare and collate various data sources: Department for Education and Employment records of participation in government-supported education and training; Careers Service pupil destinations surveys; the Labour Force Survey; and the

Youth Cohort Study. These data-sets have different strengths and do not always arrive at precisely equivalent figures. Broadly speaking, however, they allow us to calculate a residual group of non-participants to within one or two percentage points: 7 per cent of 16 year olds and 8-9 per cent of 17 year olds (Robinson, 1998).

Local analyses

Local analyses tend to show figures for non-participating young people far in excess of either official local figures or of estimates drawn from national data-sets. Why is this? To begin with there is no longer a claimant count of unemployed 16 and 17 year olds. Since 1988, 16 and 17 year olds have been disallowed from claiming benefits (except in special circumstances) and have instead been offered the 'guarantee' of a Youth Training, or the alternatives of a Modern Apprenticeship or another government-supported training place. At a local level, those young people registered with the Careers Service and awaiting a training place are referred to as the 'guarantee group' and constitute one official estimate of the numbers not participating in education, training or employment.

Research in South Glamorgan (Istance et al, 1994) found that at any one time between 16 per cent and 23 per cent of 16 or 17 year olds were in 'Status Zero'. This was well in excess of the 'guarantee' group, which represented between 1.5 per cent to 4.5 per cent of the age group, and Careers Service figures for those registered at any time in the year as seeking work or training (between 5 per cent and 12.5 per cent of the age group). It was a dynamic group, with the majority of young people experiencing some activity during the period. Nevertheless, six in ten of the group were in 'Status Zero' for more than 6 months.

The follow-up study in Mid Glamorgan (Istance et al, 1996) estimated that between 16 per cent and 20 per cent of 16-17 year olds were in 'Status Zero' at any one time. Of these, 38 per cent experienced 'Status Zero' for 6-19 months, and a further 16 per cent experienced it continually throughout the research period. Again, these figures contrast dramatically with the guarantee group – the latter showed that between 1-2 per cent of 16-17 year olds were out of education, work or training. Other local studies in the North-West and South-West of England have shown that young people change tracks frequently, moving in and out of, and between, Youth Training, further education, school, employment and unemployment (Unwin, 1995; Hodkinson *et al*, 1996). For example, in Cheshire, 18 per cent of the young people who chose to stay on in full-time education had left that route by the end of one year, many of these changing route again between one and six times.

Local versus national

The validity of the estimates that emerge from local analyses is open to question. The estimates are arrived at by adding onto the number of those in the training guarantee group two further sets of young people: those who were registered with the Careers Service at school but are subsequently 'missing' from destinations records; and those who have registered with the Careers Service as unemployed but are seeking work or training at any one time, and for whom monthly records are incomplete (that is 'missing' for some part of their 16th and 17th years).

Both of these statistical steps are problematic. First, those missing from Careers Services records cannot all be assumed to be in the non-participant group, rather than distributed across other categories. Assuming the latter is the case for national statistics produces results which are approximately complementary with other data-sets (Robinson, 1998). Secondly, the stock of non-participants cannot simply be inflated by adding the flow of those who experience unemployment at any one time.

This is not to say that official statistics, least of all the numbers represented by the guarantee group, present a complete picture. In important respects, official data sources are incomplete. There are significant areas of activity for which only limited or sample data exists. In particular, there is no on-going information on the economic activity status of young people not in education or training and the nature of any employment.[7] Moreover, TECs record weekly 'starts' so it is difficult to get a stable picture of how many young people are engaged in the work-based routes at any one time, and these local figures are difficult to translate into national ones for the DfEE. There are further problems at the local level about the different agencies sharing accurate information.

Leaving aside the problems set out above, local studies present a richer and potentially more valuable picture of non-participation in education, training or work than can be supplied by national data sources. However, as the Education and Employment Select Committee has recognised: 'more accurate information is vital if we are to grasp the true nature and extent of the problem' (Education and Employment Select Committee, 1998:xi).[8]

Key characteristics of non-participants

What then are the key characteristics of those young people not participating in education, training or employment after leaving school? Using the latest data from the Youth Cohort Study and other sources, we can identify these characteristics under the following headings:

- GCSE attainment

- socio-economic group

- housing

- family circumstances

- ethnic background

- gender

- learning difficulties and/or disabilities

Each of these is now examined.

GCSE attainment

Attainment at 16 is the strongest predictor of both future participation in education and labour market prospects. As Table 3.3 shows, those not in education, training or work are on average the least qualified group of school-leavers. Those with no or very low grades are much more likely to fall into the excluded category.[9] The latest YCS data also suggests that the dip in participation in full-time education and training which has taken place since 1993 has occurred mostly among those young people with GCSEs at Grades D-G and those with no qualifications. Participation among those with GCSEs at higher grades has held up.

These findings are broadly confirmed in local studies. Researchers in Northern Ireland found that 20 per cent of those with fewer than 2 passes at GCSE experienced long-term 'Status Zero', compared to 8 per cent of those with 3-6 passes and only 4 per cent of those with 7 or

Table 3.3: Main activity of 16 year olds by GCSE attainment, Spring 1996 (England %)

	5+ A*-Cs	1-4 A*-Cs	5+ D-Gs	1-4 D-Gs	No grades	All
Full-time education	92	68	49	34	26	71
Government training	3	13	24	22	20	11
Full-time employment	2	9	12	13	17	7
Excluded	3	10	15	30	38	9
Total	100	100	100	100	100	100

Source: YCS Cohort 8, Sweep 1;
Note: 'excluded' includes the unemployed, the inactive and a small number (1-2%) in part-time work.

more passes (Armstrong *et al*, 1997). In Mid-Glamorgan, researchers found that 43 per cent of those with no graded results moved directly into 'Status Zero' on leaving school. They concluded that:

> Status 0...requires a focus on lower attainers. There is a clear relationship between examination results and the likelihood of young people being in an unemployed or unknown destination at this early stage in their post-school 'careers'. Lack of success in gaining qualifications at school shows up almost immediately therefore as very early adult, economic, and social marginalisation (Istance & Williamson, 1996: 17).

This evidence shows clearly how GCSE (and particularly the attainment of grades C and above) is the gateway to inclusion or exclusion, and reinforces the imperative that targets are set for the success of *all* pupils.

Socio-economic group

As attainment at 16 is higher among those from higher socio-economic groups, so too is participation in education and training after leaving school. As Table 3.4 shows, those with parents in manual occupations are significantly more likely to be in government-supported training or not in education, training or work. The YCS data also suggests that the recent decrease in participation in full-time education and training has been more apparent among those with parents in manual occupations.

Table 3.4: activities of 16 year olds by father's occupation, Spring 1996 (England, %)

Socio-economic group	Managerial, prof., tech.	Service occupations	Manual occupations	Total
All	**32**	**13**	**56**	**100**
All those in education & training	34	13	53	100
Full-time education	38	13	49	100
Government training	14	13	72	100
In employment	23	13	64	100
All those not in education & training	12	10	79	100
In employment	12	12	76	100
Not in employment	11	8	80	100

Source: Derived from YCS Cohort 8, Sweep 1

Housing

Linked to socio-economic background, there is also evidence that type of housing is strongly related to exclusion from education and employment. A study for the Joseph Rowntree Foundation found that 22.6 per cent of 16-17 year olds in council housing and 28.5 per cent of housing association tenants were 'Status Zero', compared to 11.4 per cent in mortgaged property (Coles et al, 1998).

Family circumstances

Aside from socio-economic background, differences in participation also arise on the basis of the different family circumstances of young people, with similar patterns to those of excluded pupils. Those not in education, training or work are more likely than their peers to live with neither parent. Young people living with neither parent make up 4 per cent of the age group but 17 per cent of those outside education, training or work.

There is considerable evidence that young people with difficult or disturbed family backgrounds feature disproportionately amongst those who do not participate in education, training or work. Local studies reveal traumatic life histories including parental separation, bereavement, chronic illness, alcoholism and abuse (Istance et al, 1994, 1996; Armstrong et al, 1997).

Again, those currently or formerly in local authority care are particularly vulnerable (Baldwin *et al* in McDonald ed, 1997; Coles, 1995). The educational disadvantage suffered by those in care is such that they are far less likely to participate in full-time education and training after leaving school. Moreover, as we noted earlier, transition into the labour market coincides with aftercare accommodation transitions and/or problematic entry into the housing market. Their routes into adulthood are marked by an unstable environment of unemployment and frequent housing movement (Baldwin *et al* in McDonald ed, 1997). Whilst social services can offer support up to the age of 21, most young people are discharged from care between 16 or 18 and lose touch with social services shortly thereafter.

Domestic instability may be both a cause and a function of non-participation. Homelessness features disproportionately amongst the young non-participating population, although the circumstances and activities of the young homeless are far from homogeneous (Jones in McDonald ed, 1997). So too do frequent moves which disrupt a young person's school career and position within the peer group (Devlin, 1995; Wilkinson, 1995).

Ethnic background

There are clear differences between ethnic groups in the propensity to stay on in education and training. Black and Asian young people are more likely than their white counterparts to stay in full-time education, and to do so at colleges of further education rather than schools. Young white people are more likely to enter the labour market directly than all other ethnic groups apart from Bangladeshis, who are over-represented amongst those who do not receive education and training after school (Labour Force Survey). In many areas there are extremely high levels of unemployment amongst Afro-Caribbean youths, even as high as 50 per cent.

Gender

Young women are more likely to continue in full-time education or training at 16 than young men. However, the rates converge when young people reach age 17. This is largely because occupations which have traditionally recruited young women, such as clerical and secretarial jobs, do so at 17 or 18, typically after young women have spent some time in full-time education.

The problems faced by young women not in education, training or work experience tend to be obscured by the attention given to their young male counterparts. In fact, the proportions of those not in education, training or work do not differ markedly between the sexes. More young men are likely to be unemployed, whilst young women are more likely to be caring for dependants or economically inactive. At the end of 1996, some 23,000 young people (16-19 year olds) were inactive because of domestic and caring responsibilities (Labour Force Survey). Of this sizeable group, often ignored by policy-makers, most but not all were women. Given the tendency of the media and politicians to focus on under-achievement and non-participation amongst males, these points should not be ignored.

Learning difficulties and/or disabilities

Young people with learning difficulties and/or disabilities are over-represented amongst those not participating in education and training. They are not a homogeneous group: they may be defined as having special educational needs (in some cases profound and multiple), emotional or behavioural difficulties, or physical disabilities. As we have seen, however, these categories may function in certain cases as devices to discipline or segregate young people. Special further education and training may also perpetuate exclusion. Many disabled young people consequently experience prolonged transitions after leaving school, which often result in exclusion from the labour market and continued dependence on their families (Baldwin *et al* in McDonald ed., 1997).

Changes in the youth labour market

It would appear reasonable to assume that participation (and non-participation) in full-time education or government-supported training of 16-19 years olds is strongly influenced by conditions in the youth labour market. Participation in full-time education and training programmes increases when the youth labour market is depressed, as it did between 1979 and 1983 (for education and training as a whole), and after 1990 (specifically for full-time education). Conversely, where the labour market offers opportunities for early entry, particularly for those with lower levels of educational attainment at 16, then participation in full-time education or training programmes has remained flat or declines, as it did between 1984 and 1988 (Green & Steedman, 1996: 9).

According to such an account, the rise of youth unemployment in the late 1970s disrupted established school-to-work transitions, and since the mid-late 1980s, there has been a sharp decline in the proportion of young people entering the regular labour market after leaving school. Some commentators argue that the demand for youth labour has declined to such an extent that there is no longer an identifiable youth labour market (Skilbeck *et al*, 1994: 234). For this reason, rising participation rates in full-time education are held to be a consequence of youth unemployment, leaving a residual group to engage in government-supported training schemes, find low-skilled work or drop out altogether.

However, the correlation between youth labour market conditions and participation rates in education and training programmes does not hold consistently. The most important period of expansion of full-time participation rates was in the late 1980s and the early 1990s. Conditions in the youth labour market were buoyant for a large part of this period. A further problem with the correlation between the labour market and education participation is that the considerable local and regional variations in participation in post-compulsory education and training are difficult to explain. The South East has high staying-on rates, despite the greater availability of opportunities in the youth labour market, whilst participation in full-time education is lower in the North, where youth unemployment is relatively high. Consequently, it does not appear plausible to read off rising full-time participation rates against declining youth employment. In fact, the most important explanation for the rise appears to be the introduction of GCSEs in 1987/8 (Robinson, 1998).

However, at the margin, economic conditions do have an influence on the paths taken by young people who hold limited qualifications and there have clearly been changes in the youth labour market which have affected this group:

● the share of employment in traditional manufacturing industries which recruited heavily from school-leavers has declined;

● service occupations, including personal services, have grown and account for an important proportion of young people recruited into the labour market, usually after a period spent in further education or training after school;

●   unskilled and semi-skilled jobs for young people may also remain available, and when conditions in the youth labour market improve, those with poor or limited qualifications may choose to get a job directly, rather than go into full-time education or onto government-supported training schemes (Robinson, 1998).

Furthermore, the youth labour market also has an impact on those in full-time education, which is now becoming a more flexible concept. Indeed, some young people in full-time education spend as much time again in part-time work. In particular, certain sections of retailing like supermarkets rely heavily on youth labour in the evenings and at weekends.

Finally, we should also not overlook the short-term attractions of the informal, and sometimes illegal, labour markets. Education and training require deferred gratification; immediate gratification can be secured through engagement in the informal economy, which has proliferated in recent years, especially around the drugs culture. So, for many young people, it is not just the disincentives of remaining within, or sustaining application within, formal systems, but the corresponding incentives to become involved in informal systems. Within some communities, these already provide clear and visible pathways, often with more attractive and better structured opportunities in the foreseeable future.

Conclusion

Young people outside of education, training or work are not a stable group. Their circumstances are likely to change during their immediate post-school years. They are more likely to have limited school-leaving qualifications or none at all, be from lower income households, and often come from disrupted or disturbed homes. Contrary to conventional wisdom, they are fairly evenly distributed between males and females, although their experiences will vary according to gender, and they differ in the paths they follow according to their ethnicity. Amongst them are overlapping groups of extremely vulnerable young people: those leaving care, the homeless, and those with disabilities and/or learning difficulties.

It is clear from the statistical picture that there are significant numbers of 16-19 year olds (as with 14-16 year olds) that at any one time are effectively excluded from education and training, as a result of under-achievement, non-participation and disaffection. These numbers are worryingly large, and are associated with such a range of disadvantages as to constitute a major and urgent focus for policy-makers. However, young people move in and out of different categories of participation in both education and the labour market. There is not a static or empirically identifiable youth underclass. Consequently, there is considerable scope for policy intervention to turn round the lives of many of those who have achieved little at school or beyond.

Chapter 4: Strategies for tackling under achievement and disaffection in the existing education system

In this chapter, we present an overview of what works, both in prevention and amelioration of disaffection, and in raising achievement for those who fall outside of learning. Chapters 5 to 7 will examine wider reforms of qualifications, institutional arrangements and funding systems. This chapter focuses on practices and initiatives within existing frameworks:

- effective discipline;

- pupil participation;

- parental involvement;

- action to reduce truancy;

- action to reduce exclusions;

- curriculum modification;

- use of the Careers Service;

- focus on young people in care;

- inter-agency partnership.

A section at the end of the chapter suggests some further radical ways forward.

Effective discipline

Effective discipline or behaviour management is to a large extent determined by the skill of individual teachers, and there is a clear role that teacher training, induction and in-service training can play in helping teachers to control classrooms. However, effective discipline is also affected by a whole range of other factors, including school, LEA and national government policy, and of course parents and the home.

Whole-school policy

Schools are more effective in raising achievement, tackling disaffection and providing inclusive education if they have clear policies and apply them consistently. Effective discipline in schools is not a bolt-on to teaching practice. Nor is it something to be addressed to a small proportion of disruptive pupils. As the influential Elton Report (DES, 1989) argued, effective discipline is a matter of whole-school policy. A clear whole-school policy should include:

● systems of incentives, sanction and support

● shared understanding and mutual support among members of a school staff

● regular opportunities for talking matters over with students

● appropriate curriculum content and teaching styles

● effective home/school relationships

In practice, schools choose from a number of these and other strategies in order to develop behaviour policies. Effective schools provide clear and consistently enforced rules, promote good pupil-teacher relationships, strive to integrate pupils, and value all forms of achievement. Poor schools have an uncertain ethos and unclear or inconsistently applied rules. They tend to shift the blame for disaffection onto pupils and shift the responsibility for their well-being onto outside agencies.

Positive reinforcement

School effectiveness research (Sammons et al, 1995) has shown that positive reinforcement of discipline, through rewards, clear rules and other incentives, is more effective than punitive measures in the promotion of good behaviour. Currently, the government is cautiously promoting a theory and practice of behaviour management known as Assertive Discipline (DfEE, 1997g). It is based on principles of behaviourist psychology and involves the following key features (Cohen et al, 1996: 335):

● expectations of pupils' behaviour are clearly set out by the teacher;

● specific, concrete and verbal praise and rewards are given for behaviour that meets established expectations;

● there is a graded sequence of negative consequences of undesirable behaviour;

●   the teacher is assertive and consistent in the application of rewards and sanctions;

●   power resides with the teacher, while informed choice resides with the pupil.

Supporters of Assertive Discipline argue that it has achieved demonstrable success. Clear rules promote good behaviour and the use of regular praise helps to create a culture of achievement amongst pupils. But Assertive Discipline is not without its critics, who argue that its behaviourist roots underpin an unhealthy instrumentalism and a fundamental denial of the agency and subjectivity of young people. They also argue that by reducing our understanding of individual pupils to patterns of observable behaviour, Assertive Discipline neglects the circumstances of disruptive behaviour. This in turn heightens a sense of unfairness on the part of pupils and deflects attention from the fundamental causes of problems. It has even been described as inflexible, demeaning and insulting (Robinson & Maines quoted in Cohen *et al*, 1996).

Whether or not a school subscribes formally to Assertive Discipline, most clear and consistent behaviour policies are likely to have most or many of its features. Effective schools are also likely to use such a framework with flexibility, recognising that pupil-teacher relationships are key to discipline and achievement, that bullying and negative peer pressures require a particular focus, and that praise, rewards and sanctions need to be applied with particular care to very disturbed young people.

Behaviour Support Plans

In the immediate future, the most significant development for school discipline policies will be the provision of behaviour support by LEAs under the terms of the Education Act 1997 (DfEE, 1998). As from April 1998, LEAs have been required to draw up Behaviour Support Plans, linked to Children's' Services Plans and Education Development Plans, and publish them by the end of the year. These must set out arrangements for strategic planning of provision for pupils with behavioural difficulties, plans for effective inter-agency work, support for schools in the management of pupil behaviour, and support for pupils, both inside and outside the mainstream. Excluded pupils must be tracked so they can return to mainstream classes. This is potentially an important development since for the first time, behaviour support will be addressed systematically on a countrywide basis.

Pupil participation

As was discussed in Chapter 2, teacher-pupil relationships are a key determinant of the extent of disaffection. Young people specifically identify teachers treating them with a lack of respect as having a negative impact on their attitudes to school and their motivation to learn (Keys & Fernandes, 1993). Schools need to foster an environment of mutual respect between pupils and staff, in which pupils are enabled and encouraged to express their views, confident that they will be listened to politely and constructively by staff and other pupils.

Of particular proven value are mechanisms for pupils' participation in the life of the school, and particularly in decisions that affect them. There are at least three ways in which we might understand the value of pupil participation:

- increasing motivation by making young people feel more control over their time and experience at school;

- using pupil perspectives as feedback to inform teaching and learning for the individual and school improvement as a whole;

- reflecting levels of responsibility that many pupils have in their lives outside school.

The importance of pupil participation was noted by the Elton Report and has been demonstrated in studies of unusually effective schools in disadvantaged areas (National Commission on Education, 1996). In many cases schools have school or pupil councils which enable the pupils themselves to be instrumental in the development in the rules and ethos of the institution. A key implication of the interim report of the Advisory Group on citizenship education chaired by Professor Bernard Crick (QCA, 1998) is that these councils, and ways of involving a wider range of pupils in a wider range of decisions, help young people to learn by experience to be active citizens.

Moreover, in relation to the previous section on discipline, individual and whole group behaviour standards which are determined on the basis of consultation and negotiation with pupils themselves can help secure wider commitment and observance. One particular school, Highfield Junior School in Plymouth, combines pupil participation with elements of Assertive Discipline (Highfield Junior School, 1997). Once a clear set of boundaries within which behaviour can improve have been established, further negotiation and development of expectations and rules are shared within decision-making forums.

Parental involvement

Improved integration of parents into school life can pay dividends for preventing or ameliorating disaffection. Moreover, research shows that regular parental involvement and review, and guidance in relation to homework, increases educational performance. Parental involvement tends to be much stronger in primary schools, and school policy in this area is more actively aimed at parents with young children, and not those with teenagers. This is understandable: intervention is more limited in scope and less effective after problems have become entrenched or endemic.

However, the importance of child-parent relationships to the incidence and subsequent mediation of disaffection is such that parental involvement strategies are critical at all stages. In particular, parental involvement in the induction of pupils into secondary school has been shown to reduce truancy in later years. Greater parental involvement also puts a premium on clear and consistent school policies, particularly for homework and discipline, but it also requires both sensitivity and efficient use of that most valuable resource – teacher time.

Home-school links

Home-school links are a linchpin of effective action to tackle disaffection. In order to secure greater parental involvement in, and responsibility for, the education of their children the government has stated its intention to make the use of written home/school agreements mandatory (but not legally binding). These agreements will 'reflect the respective responsibilities of home and school in raising standards, explaining clearly what is expected of the school, of the parent and of the pupil' (DfEE, 1997g: 54). If properly and carefully introduced, they should become useful tools in the development of greater and more effective home-school dialogue and exchange, although great care will be needed in identifying sanctions for parents.

Home-school agreements and other measures for strengthening links between parents and schools are also important since they can help notify teachers of changes in parental circumstances – such as bereavement, separation or unemployment – which may impact on a young person's education. Likewise, changes in a pupil's behaviour patterns can be reported quickly to parents and common approaches to behaviour and discipline can be developed between the home and school environments.

Disturbed situations

Partnership with parents is obviously most difficult in disturbed domestic situations. In these situations preventative work by children's services is far more effective than reactive crisis intervention. However, resource constraints and institutional barriers mean that – as the Audit Commission (1996) noted – social services have found it difficult to fulfil the preventative-based philosophy of the Children Act 1989. And co-ordination between education and social services is often inadequate when local authorities act as corporate parents for children in care.

There is another important recent development which is likely to have an impact on disaffected teenagers. Where young people become involved in criminal activity or fail to attend school regularly, parents might become subject to new Parenting Orders. These will require parents to attend counselling or guidance sessions and, in certain circumstances, to ensure that their children attend school regularly. Critics of the orders argue that they shift too much responsibility for youth crime onto parents without offering much in support and that they will impact most heavily on the parents of those most likely to commit offences, such as the poor or lone parents (The Children's Society, 1997).

These are valid concerns, up to a point. Enforcing parental responsibility cannot of itself repair the damaged family relationships which often lie behind inadequate parental supervision and control, nor can it deal with low levels of self-esteem which often exacerbate the problems. Moreover, research suggests that interventions exclusively into one area, such as the home, or with one actor, such as a parent, are not effective in the long term. Rather, crime prevention and reparation must take place in wider social contexts, including the school environment (Graham & Bowling, 1995), and the community (Crime

Concern, 1992). Policies to ensure that parents take more active responsibility for their children must therefore ensure co-ordination of the different agencies with an interest in young people and their families.

Action to reduce truancy

The role of parents is particularly important in reducing truancy. Parents have a legal duty to ensure school attendance but clearly do not always meet it. Schools undertake a range of activities to engage parents of pupils who attend irregularly, from chasing up absence through immediate and regular telephone calls, to drop-in advice services and parenting skills work. A number of projects funded under the truancy and disaffected pupils GEST programme (1993-1995) involved peer support for parents through regular meetings with teachers and education welfare officers and parenting groups. The evaluation of these schemes found that they were not generally expensive to establish and represented good value for money if sustained. Outreach elements, for example youth outreach workers networking schools into their communities, helped gain visibility and the trust and support of parents and others in the community (DfEE, 1995).

Of course, reducing truancy requires more than tackling relations between schools and parents. The Social Exclusion Unit recently set out a range of proposals aimed at reducing the amount of time lost to truancy by a third by the year 2002 (Social Exclusion Unit, 1998). The key recommendations were:

- local authority targets set in their Education Development Plans, more demanding for the poorer performers;

- targets for particular schools with attendance records significantly below average;

- school-level data on attendance to be published;

- truancy to be a key focus of bids for Education Action Zones;

- consideration of the introduction of more work-related learning into Key Stage 4;

- better liaison between LEAs and magistrate courts;

● Courts to be able to impose Parenting Orders on parents of persistent truants;

● police to be given the power to pick up truants and return them to school or designated place.

Action to reduce exclusions

The Government has categorically stated its belief that the national rate of exclusion is too high, and that action is necessary to bring it down (DfEE, 1997). While the extraordinary rise in the past few years has now tailed off, it is undoubtedly the case that there are far too many young people being excluded. Exclusion from school is not just a consequence of disaffection. It also contributes to young people feeling rejected by the education system, to major disruption in their school careers, and, as hard evidence shows, to underachievement and a range of social problems.

As a tempting response to the competitive climate in which schools now operate exclusion is over-used, with many schools excluding pupils for inappropriate reasons (even for relatively minor transgressions such as body-piercing or unsuitable clothing). As an ultimate sanction exclusion is a necessary evil, and the majority of schools do not take the decision to exclude a pupil lightly. It is most often used as a last resort tactic to prevent the disruption of the education of other pupils, and in some extreme cases to preserve the safety of pupils and teachers. However, a key element of any overall strategy to tackle disaffection is for schools and LEAs to reduce the number of exclusions.

School action

As was discussed earlier, rates of exclusion vary hugely between schools. Those with relatively low rates employ a range of strategies in order to maintain, as far as possible, inclusive education. In addition to effective, clear and consistent behaviour policies, schools which successfully reduce exclusions provide high quality pastoral and specialist support to pupils, but also have an approach which takes account of the family circumstances of the pupil. OFSTED inspections suggest that good schools recognise the importance of tutoring, continuity and co-ordination of support and clear routes for referrals. In contrast to this, OFSTED has found that most support to students with behavioural problems tends to be reactive, disciplinary and seldom sufficiently linked to learning, rather than planned and rooted in a diagnosis of pupils' learning difficulties (OFSTED, 1996: 20). Where exclusion is being considered, schools with low rates tend to have clear, consistent and open procedures for case conferences and mediation.

LEA action

As was shown in Chapter 2, there are also wide variations in rates of exclusion between LEAs. The influence of LEAs on the policies and practices of schools is more limited now than it was but their performance in contributing to reduced rates of exclusion is improved when they:

● offer advice and procedural support;

● maintain properly co-ordinated support services,

● provide resources for staff training;

● engage in targeted work for children disaffected around the time of transfer from primary school to secondary school;

● provide or encourage out-of-school provision for under-achieving pupils, for example summer literacy programmes;

● ensure co-ordination and collaboration across local government services (for example with social workers) and by the construction of wider partnerships in the community (as will be discussed later).

Another important consideration in reducing exclusions is recognition of groups that are more at risk than others, identification of the causes of this, and then development of specific measures to address those causes. Effective LEAs are well-placed to take this on as is shown in the example overleaf.

Effective LEAs engage in detailed monitoring and analysis of comprehensive information, and use data to inform dialogue with schools. Few schools have clear arrangements in place to monitor exclusions, and monitoring and analysis is far less developed for the incidence of fixed-term exclusions and for those who are in the care of the authority, than for permanent exclusions. These are consequently important areas for agreed action and improvement between schools and local authorities in the development of Behaviour Support Plans.

Birmingham LEA: Action to Reduce Exclusions Amongst Afro-Caribbean Boys

In 1994, Birmingham LEA decided to take action to reduce exclusions amongst Afro-Caribbean boys (in 1995/6, 34 per cent of all exclusions were amongst black pupils who comprised only 9 per cent of the school population). A high-profile working party was set up and a single team appointed to work on exclusions.

The working party agreed that community initiatives such as the KWESI mentoring project should be encouraged. KWESI recruits and trains mentors from the community. Afro-Caribbean pupils excluded from schools, or at risk of exclusion, are referred to KWESI by the LEA's exclusions team.

The LEA also adapted an American programme promoted by the Coca Cola Foundation which aims to improve behaviour amongst teenagers through entrusting them with responsibility for helping younger children. The Birmingham Second City Second Chance programme has been running for two years and involves around 100 secondary school pupils, many of whom are from ethnic minorities, in tutoring primary school pupils. The secondary pupils receive vouchers as rewards.

In the first two terms of 1996/7, exclusions were down by 23 per cent from the same period a year earlier. Some 60 per cent of the reduction was amongst ethnic minority groups.

Source: DfEE Draft Guidance on LEA Behaviour Support Plans (1997)

The draft guidance issued to LEAs for the development of Behaviour Support Plans suggested that authorities should consider the use of performance indicators to assess the effectiveness of their provision. Care will be needed to avoid perverse effects on behaviour and achievement and it is unlikely that indicators will be able to capture measures of attitude, except very crudely. However, targets concentrate effort on key objectives and allow schools and local authorities to be judged on their performance. Where LEAs can collect the required information on a voluntary or statutory basis, performance targets should be set to cover:

- higher standards of achievement for pupils with behavioural difficulties, including higher standards of achievement in PRUs;

- reductions in the number of permanent and fixed-term exclusions, including targets for particular groups over-represented in exclusion figures such as those in care and ethnic-minority pupils;

- reductions in the number of persistent truants;

- increases in the number of excluded pupils and chronic non-attenders reintegrated into mainstream education within specified time-scales.

These performance measures would contribute to meeting the nation-wide target for a reduction in the number of young people leaving school without qualifications. In addition, our analysis of the institutional factors which have contributed to the rise in exclusions suggests that strategies for reducing the numbers of pupils excluded would be supported by:

- school performance indicators which provide incentives to raise the levels of achievement of all pupils, including the lowest attainers, and not just those capable of achieving 5 A*-C grades at GCSE;

- financial incentives for schools which provide admission to pupils who have been excluded, and for schools which achieve success with previously excluded pupils.

National policy

Many of the issues relating to exclusion that have been discussed in this report have been recognised by the Social Exclusion Unit. This unit recently set out a range of proposals aimed at reducing the numbers of both permanent and fixed-term exclusions by a third by the year 2002 (Social Exclusion Unit, 1998). The key recommendations were:

- local authorities to set targets in their Education Development Plans which are more demanding for the poorer performers;

- schools to notify LEAs of all fixed-term exclusions;

- major research study on reasons (and their seriousness) for exclusion;

- collection of aggregate data on achievement of those educated out of school;

- publication of secondary exclusions data by school level, and primary exclusions by LEA level, including ethnic breakdowns;

- statutory guidance on exclusions focusing particularly on best practice for prevention;

- LEAs to be given the right to be represented and heard at governors meetings;

- consultation on preventing the use of exclusion being used as a device to distort performance in league tables;

- special OFSTED inspections of ten schools with disproportionately high levels of exclusions or truancy and the right for LEAs to trigger this process;

- exclusions issues to be a key focus of bids for Education Action Zones;

- targeted partnership funds for preventative work and for schools with excluded children;

- equal opportunities issues and behaviour management to be adequately incorporated into teacher training requirements;

- promotion of community mentoring in ethnic minority communities;

- targets for the educational attainment of children in care;

- obligation on LEAs to provide every young person excluded for more than three weeks with appropriate full-time education.

Curriculum modification

A number of schools around the country experiment with curriculum modification and enhancement in order to overcome the problems of demotivation and low levels of achievement associated with the demands and content of the National Curriculum at Key Stage 4, although league tables have discouraged schools from doing so. Such curricular initiatives vary in scope, ranging from efforts to provide alternative forms of learning activity for those at risk of disaffection to highly structured course options for hard-core non-attenders and those who have been permanently excluded.

Work-related learning

At the less intensive end of the spectrum, in most cases, use is made of vocational options and extended work experience. The focus is often on short, achievable, project-based approaches which are relevant to the pupil and present attainable objectives. In some cases, alternative curriculum provision can also involve professional support from educational welfare officers, educational psychologists or youth workers.

Until recently, these approaches have been limited by the constraints of the National Curriculum. This has led the government to consult on proposals to open up opportunities for the wider use of work-related learning, both within and beyond the National Curriculum, at Key Stage 4. In response to the success of local initiatives in using work-related learning to motivate disaffected pupils, the government has sought to give schools greater flexibility to find effective ways of encouraging pupils to learn by allowing 'disapplication' of programmes of study in up to two National Curriculum subjects, excluding specified core subjects. These measures also form part of the proposed flexibility available to participants in Education Action Zones.[10]

Bridge and Link provision

Curriculum modification and enhancement for young people with serious problems of disaffection, for example those that have been excluded, usually takes the form of Bridge or Link provision. This is often offered with the involvement of voluntary agencies in partnership with schools, local authorities, further education colleges and local employers. The most effective Bridge Courses are those premised on the principle that reintegration into mainstream education and training environments should be the ultimate objective (for a good example see panel on Include overleaf). This ensures that opportunities for individual achievement and progress are paramount. The alternative – particularly in PRUs – is too often 'holding provision', in which expectations are low and standards poor.

Include: Bridge Course

Include (formerly Cities in Schools) is a national charity which works in around 25 LEAs in England and Wales with young people who have school attendance and behavioural problems. It aims to secure reintegration of young people into mainstream education and training. An important part of its work is the Bridge Course it offers to pupils at Key Stage 4.

Objectives

● assist young people to improve their literacy, numeracy and life-skills and to develop constructive leisure interests;

● provide positive learning/educational experiences for their final year of schooling;

● assist young people in exploring career options and help equip them for the realities of a working environment;

● prepare young people for independence;

● help young people achieve broadly-based and relevant training which leads to an approved qualification, thus enabling them to achieve progression into further education, training and/or employment.

Methods

● multi-disciplinary project manager assigned to groups of ten young people at a time;

● two days at FE college focusing on basic skills;

● two days relevant work experience;

● one day working with a group tutor involving personal tutorials, group work and leisure activities.

Outcomes

● 80 per cent progression to further education, training and employment;

● 80 per cent attendance rates;

● accreditation of literacy, numeracy and other skills.

Rathbone CI: Corby outreach project

Rathbone CI is a national charity and voluntary organisation formed in 1995, following a merger of two charities specialising in helping young people with special educational or training needs and unemployed adults. It is involved in government training programmes and works in partnerships with other agencies, helping people improve their basic skills, achieve vocational qualifications and move into employment. The Corby outreach project is an example of a Rathbone programme aimed at socially excluded 16-25 year olds.

Objectives

- providing access to a wide range of learning opportunities which young people see as achievable and relevant to the labour market;

- providing a 'no blame' environment in which asking for support and admission of failure is acceptable;

- overcoming deeply entrenched negative views of education and training.

Methods

- basic skills training for literacy, numeracy and IT;

- personal and social skills training, counselling and mentoring, to improve confidence and raise awareness;

- work-related skills and experience including training in partnership with a local college and Rathbone CI's own centre.

Outcomes

- 63 per cent positive progression (reintegration to FE, training and employment);

- accreditation of basic, key and vocational skills;

- development of a strong partnership between Corby Borough Council and Rathbone CI.

The critical success factors of out-of-school provision for disaffected young people include:

- personal support for students from trusted staff, such as project leaders and mentors, particularly for young people in care;

- learning plans tied to well structured programmes with clear progression routes;

- accreditation of learning achievement;

- learning in new and adult locations such as colleges and the workplace;

- committed and competent staff and high student-staff ratios;

- genuine inter-agency partnership.

A number of these are worthy of particular attention, and are dealt with elsewhere. It is also important to consider more flexible approaches to meeting the needs of excluded young people who very often mistrust established agencies. One such approach is featured in the panel previously on the Corby outreach project.

Use of the Careers Service

The Careers Service is a linchpin between different services for young people and it has a central role to play in New Start and other initiatives. It has responsibility for ensuring that pupils are aware of their options on leaving school and that they can make informed choices for their future. This role is critical, particularly in the context of the institutional bias of schools towards recruitment into their own sixth-forms. The service also co-ordinates work experience, provides referrals to education, training and employment opportunities, and maintains pupil destination surveys.

In recent years, the Careers Service has struggled effectively to serve its client groups. Privatisation, and the specific funding and contractual arrangements established for the service, undercut links between careers officers and other agencies, and put into question their professional integrity. In structural terms, the Careers Service has had to maintain impartial information and guidance services within a competitive context of provision. Ironically, however, it is often criticised for being provider-led. Moreover, inspection reports indicate variable and often poor quality. Most significantly, disaffected young people often view the careers service with diffidence or disdain.

Reorientation of the Careers Service

The Labour government has sought to re-orientate the Careers Service towards those who are at risk of non-participation, drop-out, or making the wrong choices in education and training. This is a formidable challenge. To begin with, there are obvious limits to what can be communicated about the wider world in face-to-face interviews. And as we have seen, young people who are excluded or persistently truant from school can be extremely difficult to reach, particularly if they subsequently do not participate in post-16 education, training or work. Tracking and monitoring procedures are being considerably strengthened but there remains scope for increased effectiveness in this critical area. In particular, reliable and comprehensive information on the numbers not participating in education, training or work must as far as possible underpin local strategies.

Reconnecting those who are disconnected from official agencies requires considerable outreach activity, often in partnership with Youth Services and voluntary agencies. Young people tend to view the Careers Service as part of the complex array of official agencies and services with whom they have to negotiate. If they have negative perceptions of schools, teachers and training providers, they are likely to view the Careers Service in similar terms (Wilkinson, 1995).

To counter this perception, links can be made with open door, informal entry points for disconnected young people, often drop-in facilities, which provide a first stop on the route back into formal education and training networks. The Youth Service has an important role to play here, particularly for gateway and advice provision. Alternatively, links with other statutory agencies can be used: for example working with the Benefits Agency to issue an invitation on the back of a Girocheque to call the Careers Service. Education and Business Partnerships providing 'compact' schemes can also improve the effectiveness of the Careers Service in schools and reduce initial drop-out levels.

Wider use of mentoring schemes will also be important to the reorientation of the Careers Service. The Mentoring Action Project, funded under the European Union's Youthstart programme, is targeted at disaffected young people and is designed to finance, support and develop the work of careers advisers from twenty Careers Services in the provision of one-to-one and group mentoring facilities, in order to help overcome lack of mutual trust and credibility between clients and providers.

As the Careers Service itself recognises, however, there is a fine balance to be struck in the reorientation of its work. It must continue to deliver an entitlement to careers education and advice to all young people. New efforts to reach disaffected and marginalised groups must represent the extension of a universal service and should not become targeted or stigmatised provision.

Focus on young people in care

The Government recently announced that it will be setting targets for the educational attainment of young people in care, provisionally that 50 per cent achieve a qualification by 2001 and 75 per cent by 2003. These could be extremely challenging targets and if they are to be met, further policies should be considered for the transition of care leavers into post-school education and training, building on current best practice.

Support during the summer months between leaving school and taking up new education and training places is often critical. Structured engagement in community activity or work placements should be the norm for each care leaver. One option which is cost effective in the long-term is residential activity, purchased by local authorities from providers such as the Prince's Trust. In addition, there should be a named member of staff with responsibility for induction of the care leaver into the receiving school, college or employer.

Second, care leavers could be offered financial incentives to participate in education and training. For example, the London Borough of Richmond offers care leavers £67 per week if they are living independently (whether or not in local authority sponsored accommodation) and are in full-time education (and can earn an extra £20 per week which is disregarded). This sum is considerably more than the weekly Income Support to which they are ordinarily entitled and offers both an incentive and a means to participate in full-time further education. In the longer-term, new systems of financial support for young people need better to reflect the pressures experienced by those leaving care.

Third, all relevant agencies should actively promote expectations of progress into advanced further and higher education and continue to provide material support for care leavers throughout participation at college or university (at present local authorities may provide such financial support but are only obliged to give advice and guidance up to the age of 21).

Inter-agency partnership

There is no shortage of initiatives and projects in both the statutory and voluntary sectors aimed at tackling problems of disaffection amongst young people. However successful these are, resource constraints, dysfunctional competition and lack of communication between agencies mean that there is a tendency towards piecemeal and short-term activity and a distinct absence of co-ordination. Consequently, pilot schemes which are driving new activity must be developed to ensure that effective models are mainstreamed in the longer term.

Voluntary agencies

Voluntary agencies like youth and community organisations often have the greatest expertise in tackling disaffection, particularly where they have developed closer links with young people themselves than statutory agencies are able to. They can often demonstrate clear educational gains from the alternatives they provide, most notably in terms of improved attendance and initial post-16 participation. However, as the Education and Employment Select Committee pointed out, many have 'not yet been subjected to any rigorous evaluation' (Education and Employment Select Committee, 1998: xxi). They also face other specific difficulties. Many suffer from resource problems and variable, often low-trust, relationships with the statutory agencies with whom they work. In the course of research for this report, interviews conducted with voluntary agencies active in the field of provision for disaffected young people suggested a number of factors which constrain the potential for effective service delivery:

● fragmentation and volatility of funding sources for projects;

● insufficient scope for flexible deployment of budgets between different local authority services;

- red tape in the negotiation of contracts;

- contract cultures which inhibit successful co-operation;

- institutional barriers and organisational inflexibility between statutory services.

Statutory agencies

The strength of voluntary sector provision is, of course, related to its singular focus on particular client groups. Statutory agencies have broader responsibilities and wider legal obligations and consequently there is often tension between the sectors. But there is also a need for better co-operation between and within statutory agencies. A consistent criticism of services for young people is lack of co-ordination between departments. We explore these issues further in Chapter 6. As in the voluntary sector, there is also a bewildering range of fragmented and volatile funding sources. From the perspective of achievement in compulsory education by disaffected and disadvantaged young people, some of the most serious shortcomings and inefficiencies involve:

- Poor co-ordination of Pupil Referral Units with mainstream provision in schools and LEA services. Inspections have shown that PRUs suffer a lack of clarity as to their place and purpose, and a general absence of policies to define their functions, admission criteria, lengths of placement and reintegration strategies (OFSTED, 1995b).

- Inadequate co-operation at all stages in the exclusion process.

- Failure to locate responsibility for young people in care (Stein, 1997). Responsibility for oversight of the educational needs of young people in care often falls between the bureaucracies of social services and education. Co-operation between social workers, carers and teachers can be fragmented and patchy, which contributes to the absence of a co-ordinated approach to raising educational achievement (OFSTED/SSI, 1995; Biehal et al, 1995).

- Insufficient contextualisation of pupil services within wider family support activities.

Partnerships

To combat these problems in the voluntary and statutory sectors, there is an increasing move to the creation of partnerships between agencies both within and across sectors, with varying degrees of success. The most successful partnerships are founded on genuine organisational relationships, often resulting in lasting change in working cultures and methods, and also more effective co-ordination of resources. Partnerships are effective when they are built on agreed objectives, a common sense of purpose and vision, and an expectation of reasonable longevity in resource allocation. Other, less successful partnerships are dominated by a lead partner and inhibited by bureaucratic and professional boundaries. Resources may simply be used to fill gaps in existing provision, which is then re-badged to meet the criteria of the latest initiative.

One of the principal recommendations of the Education and Employment Select Committee is pertinent here. The Committee proposed the establishment of local forums to co-ordinate the work of agencies concerned with provision for disaffected young people. The objectives of these forums would be to provide an environment for collaboration, to exchange good practice, to encourage the plugging of gaps, and to provide a mechanism for listening to the concerns and views of young people themselves. Such partnerships are the foundation of the Government's recent 'New Start' initiative.

The New Start Strategy: Key Features

- strategic initiative rather than a discrete programme

- focus on 14-17 year olds who are outside of learning or at risk of dropping out

- multi-agency partnership, involving TECs, local authorities, the voluntary sector, Careers Services, youth services, FE colleges, local employers and others

- bench-marking of disaffection and non-participation in the locality

- assessment of the effectiveness of local learning provision

- performance indicators for the reduction of disaffection and non-participation

---

New Start

A central plank of the rationale of the newly-launched New Start strategy for tackling disaffection and non-participation is to stimulate the development of strategic partnerships and effective inter-agency co-ordination. Funding of £10 million has been provided for three years to 17 partnerships across England in both urban and rural contexts. In the initial phase, work will be heavily research-orientated.

The way ahead

This brief review has pinpointed some critical factors in tackling disaffection and non-participation: the importance of whole-school discipline, parental involvement, action to reduce exclusions, multi-agency partnerships, and so on. There are plenty of examples of good practice in these areas which are going some way to alleviating problems. Some of the most successful recognise that the underlying causes of disaffection are deep-set and often come down to how young people relate to schools as institutions.

With this in mind, it is worth reflecting on a couple of challenging views of the education system. Ivan Illich's *Deschooling Society* (1971) was part of his radical critique of public institutions and his call for a 'deprofessionalisation' of social relations. In the book he argues that our conception of education has become limited and often distorted by its equation with the loci of the school and the classroom. Some of his ideas have been more recently revived and put into context by the English educationalist David Hargreaves (Hargreaves, 1994:14):

> Schools share a function with prisons and hospitals, namely to keep (young) people off the streets, out of harm and out of sight, and with luck in a caring environment where inmates will profit from their stay.

There is at least a kernel of truth in this rather extreme formulation, not least since Victorian schools were designed by the same architects responsible for creating institutions of social control such as prisons and workhouses. While Hargreaves might overstate the custodial function of schools, he does articulate a fundamental criticism of the education system: that it has a tendency to seal schools off from the outside world and make them too impermeable to outside influences.

There have been many examples, some of which have been described earlier in the chapter, to link disaffected young people in schools to employers and others in the local community. However, policy-makers need to be thinking through a more wholesale approach to innovation in the learning environment. They should also be more imaginative in defining and measuring achievement, broadening it out from a narrow focus on performance in examinations and in coursework.

Three related areas are now briefly examined: involving post-compulsory education institutions; opening up schools to the community and the world of work and developing these places as sites for learning; and using new technologies.

Newham College of FE's Year 11 programme

Objectives
Newham College of FE is contracted by Newham LEA to provide full- and part-time programmes for a target group of Year 11 pupils (around 90 this year) who are not entering GCSEs, who are chronic non-attenders, who have been excluded, or who have emotional and behavioural difficulties. Their schools must pay £550 towards the total £1,250 cost per pupil.

Methods
Each young person has an individual learning programme which begins with an induction phase including careers advice, occupational testing and taster courses. The rest of the programme embodies basic and key skills (for example communication, numeracy and IT) and a range of vocational programmes and work experience in areas like art and design, hair and beauty, sport and leisure, care, and technology

Outcomes
The programme has been very successful in promoting participation, achievement and progression with an extremely disadvantaged group of pupils. 70 per cent of the 142 pupils in 1996/7 had achieved firm offers for further education, youth training or employment, and most of those remaining were receiving support from the Youth and Careers Services.

Involving post-compulsory education institutions

The education system suffers from powerful barriers between different sectors, and links between them are relatively undeveloped. Where these are made, at all levels, they provide interesting opportunities for motivating young people. As we have seen, for the 14-16 year old age group the most relevant links are with the further education sector. For some of these young people, particularly those who have negative associations with school, further education colleges can provide an alternative location for learning, where they can study alongside an older age group in a mature environment, and where they can be brought into early contact with a range of post-compulsory routes as well.

There are a number of cases of colleges that have developed programmes and alternative curricular provision for 14-16 year olds. One successful example is shown in the box on the previous page.

Opening up schools to work and the community

Earlier in this chapter we discussed how work-related learning and work experience can be effective in motivating young people who are disillusioned with schooling. The next step could be a more widespread use of initiatives which break down the boundaries between schools, the world of work, and the community. Ideas include the following:

- As proposed in a previous IPPR publication, a new class of teachers – Associate Teachers – making a regular contribution to schools, over a sustained period of time, through half-day or day release schemes, secondments, or project-based work (Barber & Brighouse, 1992).

- Young people spending periods of time in companies pursuing education and training activities alongside employees (Hargreaves, 1994).

- Certain types of business units such as design studios, operating from within school buildings (Barber, 1993).

- Mentorship schemes which provide a framework in which a sustained relationship is developed with a role model from the world of work, helping young people to achieve their potential, partly through support and advice in working towards learning and other goals.

- Industry-specific curriculum initiatives for the 14-16 age group, such as the various schemes sponsored by the Construction and Industry Training Board allowing young people to gain work experience and credit towards national qualifications.

- Projects based in pupils' local communities, or curriculum initiatives organised through voluntary organisations, which connect to the citizenship agenda discussed earlier: for example, activities which challenge participants to learn from practical experience and take responsibility; which mix role models; have a strong emphasis on personal development through team-work; and which open up broader aspects of the community like the economy and environment and lead to positive learning outcomes.

As schools become opened up to the world of work and the community, options afforded by ideas like those above must strive to attain high status as broader studies or activities within a more flexible system (see Chapter 5). In the short or medium-term, it is also important that their impact on the rest of the national curriculum is held in check so that there is no danger that the school-leaving age is effectively lowered by stealth.

Using new technologies

A vast range of new forms and styles of learning are being made possible through information and communications technologies. In particular, multimedia and interactive networks enable young people to engage in learning which is exciting, innovative and not associated with traditional education. This is particularly important for those who have not been motivated by mainstream provision. The potential benefits include:

- the scope for greater differentiation of learning experiences for individual young people;

- allowing pupils access to a burgeoning array of alternative resources (particularly on the World Wide Web) to support their learning;

- enhancing the curriculum and broadening the focus of learning out from school to the world outside, including the world of work;

- enabling active participation and creative activity in exciting new forms;

- connecting young people with those in other schools locally, across the country, and abroad;

● connecting young people to people outside schools;

● removing the constraints of school structures that group pupils purely by age (and in some cases ability);

● bypassing the hierarchical relationships associated with forms of communication based on face-to-face contact;

● enabling opportunities for young people to have greater autonomy in the development of the structures and rules of their learning environments;

● allowing mistakes to be made in a less public environment.

It is early days in the use of new technologies in education. The development of the National Grid for Learning has the potential to accelerate the pace of innovation and access to its opportunities, particularly if a sensible resourcing framework is designed, and if the initiative receives sustained political support.

Learning in the New Millennium

This is a seven year project run by Ultralab at Anglia Polytechnic University and funded by Nortel. It connects young people, aged 8 to 18 years, teachers and academics with engineers in an online learning community. The young people cover the whole ability range, including those who have specific learning difficulties and the schools cross the city/rural divide. The emphasis of the project is on the production of collaborative project work in a variety of media including audio, video and animation.

The research results of this project show that breaking some of the traditional barriers present in formal education has raised the interest in learning in nearly all pupils in the project, including those who were previously viewed by the school as having few educational skills. The project is being extended in its latest phase to include those young people who, for a number of reasons (illness, bad behaviour, bullying etc.) are not permanently in school.

Pilot projects like 'Learning in the New Millennium' have already shown that new models of learning can be implemented at a surprisingly rapid pace if flexible structures for on-line learning networks are put in place. Scaling up or proliferating these models will also bring new entry and re-entry points for the young people who, for a whole variety of reasons, are rarely present in the physical buildings of schools, for example those who are ill, school-phobic, or taught at home. Given the high costs of supporting many of these pupils, it may even be an effective use of LEA budgets to equip the homes of certain young people with appropriate information and communications technologies. In the long-term policy-makers should be explore the development of 'Virtual Schools', bearing in mind that many under-achieving or disaffected young people have particular needs for personal support.

Conclusion: limitations of reform in the current education system

The low levels of achievement of so many young people in compulsory education, and subsequently intermittent participation in education, training and work after leaving school are now high on the policy agenda. There is a whole range of initiatives coming on stream which will begin to tackle many of the problems we have outlined in this report.

This chapter has examined ways in which activities within the current education system can motivate the disaffected and the non-participating. Taking next steps, however, will require a vision of long-term development in which strategies for raising participation and achievement in 14-19 education and training are inclusive, systemic and durable. In a sense, initiatives that currently succeed do so against the odds operating as they do in an inhospitable policy environment of 'fragmented often short term provision for the young people in most difficulty in our society' (Hustler *et al*, 1998: 24). The effectiveness of much of the activity in this chapter is limited by factors outside the control of local agencies: the curriculum and qualifications structure for 14-19 year olds; the whole organisational framework of education, training and other services; and the funding of learning, in particular. It is to these wider issues, and the more extensive set of reforms that must be undertaken, that we turn to in the following chapters.

Chapter 5: Qualifications, curricula and options for 14-19 year olds

Our starting point must be what young people learn and achieve. It is this which will motivate them and equip them with the knowledge, skills and understanding that will enable them to succeed in work and in life in general. This chapter therefore focuses on the curriculum, qualifications and options available to young people, and the relationship between these and under-achievement and disaffection. The existing qualifications framework is outlined, and the reforms proposed by the Dearing Review and in recent Government documents are examined. The chapter then sets out options for moving towards a more unified system of qualifications and curricula and the impact on non-participation and disaffection of these approaches is discussed. The chapter ends with an analysis of Youth Training and reform of the work-based route.

The existing qualifications framework

Qualifications for 16-19 year olds are divided into three tracks:

- the academic track of A and AS levels;

- a general vocational track, consisting of GNVQs and traditional qualifications; and

- an occupational track for those in work-based learning, geared to the attainment of NVQs.

This tripartite division has now emerged at Key Stage 4 (14-16 year olds), with the recent introduction alongside GCSEs of Part One GNVQs and use (albeit limited) of NVQ units. This framework has come under sustained criticism from employers, professionals, education and training providers and academic researchers for a number of years, chiefly because it embeds divisions between academic and vocational learning. Academic education is the 'gold standard' which offers the royal route into higher education and labour market success, whilst vocational education is lower status, second-class provision. It also generates immense confusion amongst parents, employers and pupils themselves. This systemic division also has specific effects within each of the three tracks.

The academic track

A levels are too narrow a preparation for learning throughout life, with most students taking three or fewer subjects. Britain – excluding Scotland – is the only advanced country in which students can specialise in so few subjects at such an early stage in their education. This specialisation represents a sharp break for students after the breadth of GCSEs. Within A levels, learning is limited to subject-based knowledge which defines curriculum content, rather than vice versa. Linear syllabuses and terminal assessment also inhibit access and flexibility.

The general vocational track

Broad vocational studies remain associated with lower attainers. GNVQs in particular fail to provide rigorous knowledge content or adequate preparation for either specialist employment or transfer to higher education (Spours in Hodgson & Spours eds., 1997: 57-73). From inception, GNVQs faced serious problems generated by their initial reliance on the NVQ competence-based model: bureaucratic and inadequate assessment, fragmented content, and a lack of technical rigour. They have undergone extensive revision to deal with these problems but there is still a long way to go if they are ever to gain parity of esteem with A levels. Meanwhile, take-up of traditional qualifications remains strong in both the full-time vocational education and the part-time occupational tracks, most notably the BTEC National Diploma.

The occupational track

It is a deep-set feature of the British system that applied learning is seen as inferior, and is to be taken up by those who cannot or will not be academically successful. This problem has been compounded by weaknesses with NVQs, which are too narrow and occupationally specific to provide a platform for future learning progression for young people. They suffer low take-up and attainment rates and have been repeatedly criticised on a number of grounds:

- strict competence-based philosophy leading to far too great a focus on skills needed only in the very short-term;

- jargon-ridden standards;

- complex and inadequate assessment;

- failure to develop underpinning knowledge and understanding.

The division between the three qualifications tracks – in terms of learning content, teaching methods, assessment and grading – requires students to make early choices which cannot readily be corrected if they are inappropriate. It is extremely difficult, and often impossible, for students to transfer between courses or combine options in a flexible way. The qualifications structure therefore contributes directly to high drop-out and low attainment rates, and of course to disaffection and non-participation.

The Dearing Review

The Dearing Review was established to address some of these failures in the qualifications for 16-19 year olds, for example low levels of participation and completion, incoherence and narrowness in study programmes, inflexibility in delivery, and poor attainment of core skills (Dearing, 1996). Yet it was strongly circumscribed by its terms of reference, which insisted on a consolidation, rather than potential transformation, of the existing qualifications framework.

The main recommendations

Dearing's major recommendations reflected the boundaries within which the review had been conducted:

- a more coherent national framework of qualifications, based on the three distinct pathways, with four levels of achievement from Entry level to Advanced level, to provide overarching frameworks linking attainment in the different qualifications tracks;

- National Certificates at each level to provide equivalence of academic and vocational qualifications;

- a new National Diploma at advanced level to address the narrowness of A level study;

- a new push on attainment of key skills within each of the tracks, involving certification within the new National Certificates and National Diploma, particularly to meet criticisms of over-specialisation in A level study.

- a new lateral AS level, equivalent to half an A level, to be attained after one year of study, to reduce the number of young people dropping-out without recognised achievement;

- redesignation of Advanced GNVQs as Applied A levels, and the reorganisation of the award into six units;

- consideration to be given to a three unit Applied AS to match the AS in the A level family and also to reduce drop-out;

- greater symmetry between the broad vocational and academic tracks to permit more flexibility for transfer;

- consolidation of the three tracks in terms of subject and assessment distinctiveness;

- a reform of Youth Training, linked to progression into Modern Apprenticeships;

- rationalisation of awarding and regulatory bodies;

- a set of measures to consolidate and regulate the standards of A levels.

In many ways, a key implication of the proposals was that the distinctiveness of the different tracks was to be reinforced. Dearing offered overarching certification of vocational and academic qualifications – a transparent 'wrapper' – rather than unification. In this sense, the report proposed the retention of a strongly demarcated set of tracks within a weak framework (Spours & Young, 1996).

Dearing and disaffection

As we have seen, strategies for tackling disaffection at Key Stage 4 rely heavily on the use of vocational learning. There is a long history of responding to disaffection in older age school pupils through work-related provision. Yet apart from programmes with wider objectives, such as the Technical and Vocational Education Initiative (TVEI), this activity has largely been localised, short-term, and more or less successful, depending on its scope and ambition.

The development of a national policy for vocational provision for 14-16 year olds was an additional outcome of the Dearing Review. Dearing identified under-achievers, particularly those disaffected with education, as a discrete group of young people requiring new forms of motivation beyond standard support work within the academic curriculum. He suggested that the experience of applied learning in further education should guide the development of vocational options, with hands-on work experience, for young people who had rejected the school setting and academic curriculum.

The report proposed that students should have opportunities to take approved GNVQ units at Foundation and Intermediate levels from the age of 14 onwards, as well as new Entry level qualifications. The Part One GNVQ pilots have already shown that work-related learning can be successful for pupils who have made little progress in other subjects. Given the workplace origin and design of NVQs, Dearing recognised the problem of making their use more widespread in the school context. However, he recommended consideration of which NVQ units could be taken up more widely in schools. In making these recommendations, Dearing was ratifying the existing efforts of practitioners to retain participation and raise achievement for disaffected pupils, using vocational work and links with colleges and employers.

However, at the same time, Dearing was potentially formalising and entrenching provision for disaffected pupils within the divided, tripartite system of 14-19 qualifications. The proposed use of vocational options in new settings offered disaffected pupils and under-achievers learning outside of the demotivating confines of the academic curriculum but at a cost which has traditionally been paid for such provision: the guarantee of low status and selectivity.

Dearing's proposals for disaffected 14-16 year olds illustrate the central tension for inclusive reform strategies aimed at raising achievement for all. On the one hand there is a clear need to provide relevant and achievable attainment opportunities to disaffected and disengaged young people. On the other hand it is vital to ensure that all young people are entitled to high standards within a broad and balanced curriculum.

'Qualifying for Success'

Although progress was made on some of the Dearing recommendations, the main body of the report was put on hold almost immediately after the 1997 election. The uneasy compromises in the Dearing report had begun to unravel, and practitioners and curriculum advisers objected to the prohibitively tight implementation time-scale of proposals which were increasingly seen as flawed.

The Labour government has since consulted upon a revised set of reform proposals, contained in the document *Qualifying for Success* (DfEE, 1997f). This brought together a number of strands for consultation: the government's Manifesto commitment to broaden A levels and upgrade vocational qualifications; the detail that had underpinned this commitment in the Labour Party's pre-election document *Aiming Higher*, (Labour Party, 1996); and outstanding Dearing proposals. It did not propose radical reform but instead sought views on how to improve the existing qualifications structure, with the possibility left open of more extensive reform in the longer term.

A single overarching certificate

The most important issue for consultation concerned the design of a single overarching certificate at advanced level. *Qualifying for Success* suggested that this certificate could:

- include achievements across all nationally-accredited qualifications at advanced level;

- encourage the attainment of breadth, including key skills;

- be properly structured with rules of combination for its attainment, for example depth in particular subjects;

- be differentiated and graded to act as a realistic target for most learners at advanced level, while encouraging high levels of achievement;

- be accessible to part-time learners, who should be able to build up credit towards the certificate.

The proposals for an overarching certificate in *Qualifying for Success* allowed for different interpretations – between a modified wrapper for existing qualifications to a potentially more robust diploma covering academic and vocational education. The Government is still consulting on the feasibility and desirability of a single overarching certificate. However, the consultation on the range of proposals ended with a more limited reform agenda than that potentially offered in the original set of issues for discussion. The Government has identified a number of areas in which to proceed (Blackstone, 1998):

- the development of lateral AS levels and 3 Unit Advanced GNVQs, which could act as basic building blocks for a unitised system of qualifications;

- limited modularisation and balanced assessment within A levels, slight relaxation of the restrictions on coursework, and allowing greater flexibility for progression and attainment;

- alignment of grading within A levels and GNVQs to increase symmetry between these qualifications;

- some development of an expanded concept of key skills which looks beyond the three skills of communication, application of number and information technology.

Many of these are useful steps forward. However, as we argue below, in the long-term, more extensive reform will be of fundamental importance for raising achievement amongst all young people, not least for those who are disaffected, under-achieving or not participating in learning.

Towards a unified 14-19 curriculum?

Proposals for a unified 14-19 curriculum first emerged in 1990 when the Institute for Public Policy Research published *A British Baccalaureate* (Finegold *et al*, 1990). In the years following this publication, the concept of a unified curriculum attracted considerable support, most notably from the National Commission on Education (1993).

The vision: the road to unification

A unified 14-19 curriculum would replace the existing tripartite qualifications system with a single award – perhaps an Advanced Diploma or a General Education Diploma – achieved through attainment in core and specialist studies, with specified rules of combination of units of assessment for the different learning programmes pursued by students. Learning would be organised on a modular basis, with assessment on a 'fitness for purpose' basis, covering all of 14-19 education and training, including work-based provision.

The key objectives of a unified 14-19 curriculum would be to ensure that all students achieved a breadth of attainment in different subjects and skills; that the curriculum permitted flexibility for entry and exit, progression and transfer; and that the framework of achievement was coherent and comprehensible to all. It would be based on an expansion of taught time to meet tougher demands for breadth and depth.

Since 1990, proponents of unification have recognised that the process of reform will be more complex and differentiated than originally envisaged. They have consequently developed the concept of 'steps and stages' within a broad reform strategy (Spours & Young in Hodgson & Spours ed., 1997: 206-210). These would involve movement from the track-based system, to a framework-based system, and eventually to a unified system. From an evolutionary perspective, these alternatives could be seen as stages of development in the movement from a currently divided and low performance qualifications system towards a new and unified advanced curriculum.

Step 1: Away from a track-based system

The current reform agenda offers some preliminary movement away from a rigid track-based system. The Government's response to *Qualifying for Success* builds on the Dearing proposals and in many ways offers a more coherent framework for qualifications. However, it remains limited, and in certain areas, such as modularisation, flexibility of study time, and the deferral of the overarching certificate, it puts the brakes on unification.

Step 2: A single framework for qualifications

The second step would be to create a single framework for qualifications, leading to the award of a single overarching certificate, in which rigidities between the tracks were broken down. This could be permissive, along the lines of the proposals that received support in the 1990s (for example Association for Colleges *et al*, 1994), or more prescriptive, as in the original proposals for a single certificate set out in *Qualifying for Success*. Key transitions could involve:

- creation of a three unit AS and three unit GNVQ as the main building block of the system;

- extension of modularisation and unitisation to all qualifications as the basis for common assessment structures and a credit accumulation and transfer system;

- prescribed attainment for the overarching certificate;

- mandatory attainment of key skills;

- the introduction of more levels into the National Framework in order to promote flexible progression;

- a revamped National Record of Achievement;

- inclusion of the work-based route, possibly through a vocational variant of the overarching certificate to replace GNVQ and NVQ units.

There would be a potentially wide range of learning within the framework: from existing forms of study to more flexible combinations of units from different tracks.

A single framework would permit study towards recognised qualifications but certify achievement in a single, overarching certificate at advanced level. Moreover, the development of a credit framework would go some way further in securing improved student choice, increased participation and achievement, curriculum innovation, and equivalence of learning outcomes.

Step 3: A unified system

The third and final step is the development of a fully unified qualifications structure in which the division between tracks has disappeared. This would involve departure from the single framework in several key respects. We have sketched out above what these would be: a single diploma to replace existing qualifications, starting at Key Stage 4; broader study, with a core curriculum alongside depth specialisation; forms of learning which combined the development of subject knowledge with active, project-based work; and flexibility to permit progression and recognition of attainment in building block units (Spours & Young in Hodgson & Spours ed., 1997: 206-210).

The impact on non-participation and disaffection

Evidently, curriculum change alone cannot offer a solution to the problems of disaffection, non-participation and low achievement. But it can play a critical role within a wider set of reforms. A unified system of 14-19 qualifications could help to raise achievement for 14-19 year olds, particularly the non-participating, the disaffected and the disengaged. It would potentially provide increased flexibility, greater breadth, and a genuine attempt to address the divisions in esteem in which different tracks are held by employers, providers and young people themselves.

Flexibility

A modular, unit-based 14-19 curriculum would allow personal pacing of learning, decouple qualifications from age and permit simultaneous study at different levels of the framework in accordance with the needs of the individual. This would help overcome the demotivation which results from over-prescription at Key Stage 4 and beyond, and permit recognition of attainment for small steps, with flexible entry and exit points.

Breadth

Students would study towards a wider variety of skills and knowledge in different settings: school, college, the workplace, and in the community as a whole. The curriculum would be connected in new ways to wider society and permeable to changes in the socio-economic environment. Applied knowledge could be gained alongside basic skills and broader general education.

Status and standards

Provision for disaffected and disengaged young people would no longer be 'outside' mainstream education, localised or of limited progression value. All studies would take place within a unified curriculum.

Progression

Young people, particularly those with lower levels of attainment, would no longer face a sharp break at the age of sixteen. Opportunities for progression would be seamless, and the new flexibility introduced into the curriculum and qualifications structure would permit learning across current age divides.

Youth Training and the work-based route

We have not yet addressed the key mechanisms through which many disaffected or disconnected young people can undertake vocational education after leaving school. A criticism levelled at proposals for a unified curriculum is that they neglect difficult questions that arise from inclusion of the work-based route. Indeed there are very real problems associated with bringing NVQs for young people into a unified qualifications and curriculum structure. However, reform remains imperative. Those with low attainment in compulsory education are more likely to enter jobs without training or Youth Training programmes than their peers. Their participation will often be sporadic and their experiences of the labour market are very often negative.

Youth Training

Youth Training (YT) has consistently been marked by large regional differences in participation, uneven patterns of distribution across the youth labour market, and the stratification and differentiation of opportunities (Coles, 1995; Spours, 1995). Despite efforts to rebrand and even disguise the programme, it is viewed as low status, dead-end and 'slave labour' by large numbers of those young people for whom it is designed. Furthermore, the performance of TECs in YT is impossible to judge since the league tables take no account of the different challenges faced by different TECs.

The Dearing Review reiterated many of these criticisms, noting that the association of YT with unemployment affected attitudes towards it, its status, and the qualifications associated with it. Dearing argued that some young people were motivated to participate in YT by the prospect of financial support from the State and that it is the State support itself that devalued its status. He chose not to mention the fact that the low level of the training allowance incentivises early exit into better paid jobs and that young people who are largely denied access to any state benefit have few other options. However, Dearing acknowledged poor levels of completion and attainment in YT, making particular reference to the absence of general education requirements in the programme.

Recent reforms to the work-based route

Partly in response to the points made above, a new system of National Traineeships was introduced in September 1997. The National Traineeships are programmes designed to industry standards, available from Entry to Advanced levels, incorporating NVQs and the key skills of communication, number and IT. They are underpinned by formal training agreements and designed to enable progression to Modern Apprenticeships and further work-based learning. Employee status for trainees is to be promoted wherever possible. In addition, Modern Apprenticeships are to be expanded. These reforms to the work-based route are substantial and potentially represent major advances.

To back up these reforms, the government has also legislated to give 16 and 17 year olds in work who are not in full-time secondary or further education, and have not reached NVQ level 2, the entitlement to the equivalent of day release to study towards an approved qualification. The costs of this study will be met from the public purse and are provisionally estimated at £40 million per annum.

Incorporating work-based qualifications into a unified system

Education and training in the work-based route remains geared to the attainment of NVQs at level 2, albeit inclusive of key skills. The NVQ route, as we have argued, represents an inadequate preparation for future learning or success in the labour market. This issue would be addressed by incorporation of work-based qualifications into the proposed unified system. Occupational specialisation would be pursued alongside a broader and more rigorous general education programme. For example, we could enable young people in the work-based route to continue with foundation or intermediate-level study (particularly in maths and English) and make the outcomes of the work-based route more reliable.

Such an approach would bring the English system closer to Continental models, in which technical and vocational courses have a stronger educational component. In recent years, this educational component has increased in response to the speed by which very specific occupational skills now become obsolete and the perceived need to equip young people with wider cognitive abilities for a changing labour market. However, unlike certain Continental systems, we are not proposing to retain a distinct vocational 'track'. All the experience of our education and training systems suggests that the standards and status of vocational education cannot fundamentally improve within a divided structure.

Conclusion

Our discussion of the 14-19 qualifications and curriculum systems has attempted to show that disaffected young people and those who have low levels of attainment in compulsory education are badly served by the existing qualifications structure. Vocational options are low grade, partly for reasons of quality and partly because of the polarisation of status enshrined in the qualifications system. Flexibility and opportunities for progression are limited and attainment levels are poor. The virtues of progressive movement to a unified 14-19 curriculum and qualifications structure in attempting to overcome these problems have been stressed.

Qualifications reform is invariably a complex and demanding process, as the plethora of reviews of GNVQs and NVQs has shown. It requires caution and pragmatism. However, a long-term vision of change can help guide short and medium-term reforms and give students, parents, practitioners and providers a coherent sense of the developmental process. The potential for a unified system of qualifications provides that vision, even if it remains some way off.

Chapter 6: The organisational framework of provision

This chapter examines the institutional and organisational arrangements for the provision of education and training and other services for the 14-19 year old age group. It begins by looking beyond education and it touches on the complex range of agencies providing services for disadvantaged young people. It then describes the various divisions that exist within the tertiary sector of education, the impact of the introduction of a 'quasi-market' across providers, the pressure that puts on careers advice, particularly for disadvantaged young people, and some recent and planned reforms. We end by looking ahead to how regionalisation may provide solutions to the problems identified.

Services for disadvantaged and disengaged young people

Before examining the organisation of tertiary provision, the main focus of this chapter, it is worth discussing briefly a broader range of services. There are well documented problems in the co-ordination and planning of service delivery for those young people either at risk of disaffection or suffering multiple disadvantage. But there are also some innovative attempts to tackle these problems, and, in particular, a welcome recent recognition from the Social Exclusion Unit (1998) of four issues for future examination:

- the need for integration of the multiplicity of statutory plans affecting young people and for joint audit and inspection of different services;

- the need for better information-sharing between professionals;

- training for better understanding of professional interfaces, for example for young people in care;

- joint dissemination of lessons of different departments' programmes for reducing truancy and exclusions.

Fragmentation and complexity

Services for children and young adults are delivered by a range of statutory and non-statutory agencies and departments, including purchasers or providers of education and training, health, social services, employment and benefit services. Where offences are committed, the police authorities and probation services are also involved. From an individual's point of view, the organisational and professional boundaries between and within these agencies are a web of Byzantine complexity.

Despite legislative and other efforts to ensure adequate co-ordination of services and consistency of intervention, the practical reality is that disaffected and vulnerable young people often receive fragmented and confusing services from different agencies.

Agencies and departments have different objectives, priorities and professional practice norms. In part, this reflects inadequate corporate purpose in local authorities. Although local authorities draw up formal planning arrangements and multi-agency strategies, effective service delivery across departmental boundaries remains inhibited by a range of factors including:

● rigidities in organisational structures;

● deep-set professional ideologies;

● insufficient corporate drive;

● resource constraints hampering operational capacity;

● uncertainties and discontinuities resulting from the need to bid competitively for funds;

● legislative requirements restricting flexibility and innovation in the deployment of budgets;

● inadequate funding incentives for collaboration.

The potential complexity of children's services is neatly summarised in the hypothetical scenario set out in the box below by Martin Stephenson, Chief Executive of Include (formerly Cities in Schools). The complexity described has not changed much in the two years since it is written, and the report of the Social Exclusion Unit (1998) reinforces the central point of the plethora of agencies and procedures to which many young people are subject.

Services for young people

'Each agency has bureaucratic systems processing these categories of young people into a disparate array of services. These systems all operate on an assessment-plan-review-cycle. A child with special educational needs will be subject to this process under the Education Act 1993. If this child were to be prosecuted for an offence he or she would be assessed for a Pre-Sentence Report and, if a Criminal Supervision Order were the sentence, would have a detailed plan (including education) and regular reviews. If this same child had also been subject to abuse he or she might have undergone the assessment and planning required by a Child Protection Case Conference and subsequent registration. If a family breakdown were to occur then this child might need to be looked after by the local authority. Under the Children Act this would necessitate a detailed assessment and care plan (including education) with statutory reviews. The complex if not downright confusing interplay between these processes coupled with the underlying difficulties experienced by this child could easily result in behaviour likely to lead to exclusion from school, in which case the child would be subject to the exclusion procedures laid down in the Education Act 1993.'

Source: Stephenson in Blyth & Milner eds. 1996: 251-2

Increased co-ordination within local authorities

In response to some of these problems of inter-agency service provision, innovative local authorities – particularly those starting from scratch like unitary authorities in a new era of local government – are attempting to design the organisation of services on the basis of whole-client needs. This is a trend which builds not only on the multi-agency imperatives of the 1990s but on the basis of bottom-up re-evaluation of service delivery. One example is given overleaf.

Pressure for reform of organisational structures is also likely to be driven by the compliance costs associated with new planning requirements. In order to drive up performance standards and institutionalise multi-agency partnerships, central government has subjected local authorities to extensive planning requirements in recent times. In addition to Children's Services Plans, LEAs now need to produce or contribute to Early Years Development Plans, Education Development Plans, Behaviour Support Plans, Community Safety Plans, and many more. As the Audit Commission (1998) has noted, there is a danger of 'plan proliferation'.

Milton Keynes: Action for Youth Teams

Milton Keynes Council is attempting to improve its services for young people aged 12 or over who are disaffected or at risk of becoming so, by integrating skills, knowledge and expertise from a variety of professional disciplines, and by consulting and collaborating with key services and agencies operating in the community.

Teams are being established in two areas based around school catchment areas, each consisting of a multi-disciplinary unit including social workers, youth workers, education welfare and community work staff, with direct involvement of school staff and access to other networks both within the Council (for example Arts and Leisure and Youth Justice) and outside it (for example Careers Service, the Police and local businesses), with Service Level Agreements where necessary.

These teams will undertake audits of need matched against existing provision and then prioritise preventative and supportive activity. They will then deliver some social services functions to young people, for example to those in care or on the Child Protection Register. The teams will not take formal responsibilities like procedures for persistent truants or child protection investigations. However, they will work closely with those services.

Whilst these plans seek to ensure that multi-agency co-operation becomes the norm for service delivery to key groups of young people, the longer-term objective should be to develop organisational structures and corporate performance objectives which obviate the need for detailed prescription of inter-institutional activity.

Plans will continue to be necessary for a wide range of activities, and for the formalisation of partnerships with outside agencies. However, an effective local authority will be one which institutionalises change itself and develops new working relationships with its partners. Amongst other things, this will demand more effective corporate leadership and new project-based, multi-disciplinary skills from managers and team leaders, rather than professional subject knowledge. There are, of course limits to this process, both practical, professional and legislative. But the new era of local government is witness to renewed pressure to reform service delivery: less on the basis of purchaser-provider divisions and the contracting out of provision; and more on the basis of effective performance across previously discrete and unco-operative departments. In short, services needs to be integrated and focused on the whole needs of client groups, rather than being sliced up by professional and disciplinary boundaries.

Tertiary provision

The more specific focus of this report is on education and training provision. In particular, the way that the tertiary system is organised is a key issue with a major impact on under-achievement and disaffection, and indeed on all young people.

A divided system

The division between academic, vocational and occupational education for the 14-19 age group is mirrored, and reinforced, in institutional and organisational divides. The Labour government elected in 1997 inherited a complex, fragmented and ultimately unstable institutional framework of tertiary provision. This framework had been developed by successive pieces of education and training legislation, the single most important being the 1992 Further and Higher Education Act, which removed sixth-form and further education colleges from the jurisdiction of local authorities.

Tertiary provision is currently configured as follows:

- local education authorities retain responsibility for the funding of education (mainly academic but starting to develop some vocational work) in school sixth-forms, although Local Management of Schools has reduced their degree of planning control;

- the Further Education Funding Council has responsibility for funding a wide range of academic and vocational students in sixth-form colleges and further education colleges; and

- Training and Enterprise Councils have responsibility for the funding of Youth Training/National Traineeships and Modern Apprenticeships.

Organisational structures, mechanisms of resource allocation, quality assurance and forms of accountability differ between each of these sectors. As an additional division, the Funding Agency for Schools will, until it is finally wound up, continue to fund schools which opted out of the local authority framework. This serves as a reminder that pre-16 education has also been subject to institutional division.

On the positive side of tertiary reforms over the last decade, it is generally recognised that many colleges have become more innovative, better managed and more responsive to their students since incorporation. Local authorities had a variable and often poor track record in managing and resourcing further education and many adjusted without rancour to their loss of responsibility in this area of tertiary provision. The removal of colleges from local authorities is now irreversible. Although the experience of incorporation has been a mixed one, colleges have now undergone sufficient change as to make a return to former arrangements both impractical and undesirable. Colleges now have greater scope for flexibility and innovation and they have extended their activities beyond local authority boundaries. Many have developed formal links, to the point of merger, with higher education institutions.

Moreover, LEAs themselves have changed and occupy different roles vis-à-vis schools. Compulsory education has now been set on a new institutional footing: one which preserves the delegation of powers to individual schools, refocuses the role of local education authorities towards standards and performance, and reverses some of the worst effects of the division between different types of school brought about by Conservative government reforms. This will have a knock-on effect on provision in the 14-19 age range, but LEAs are not in a position to demand or desire the return of colleges to their control.

TECs have been less successful at proving their worth and appear subject to the periodic discovery of fraudulent awards of qualifications by providers with whom they have contracted. Doubts have been persistent as to the consistency of TEC performance, the standards delivered by training providers, and the accountability of TEC boards (even with mandatory employer majorities, TEC boards have only covered a tiny proportion of local businesses).

The introduction of quasi-markets

Compounding this structural complexity, purchasers and providers of 14-19 education and training operate in a competitive environment. To this degree, tertiary provision displays features of the quasi-markets introduced more widely into public services, and replicates core principles of the paradigm of service provision developed in the 1980s and 1990s:

- competition between autonomous, corporate service providers, designed to raise levels of customer responsiveness, subordinate producer interests, and drive up efficiency;

- funding, purchasing and quality assurance delivered through quangos rather than elected authorities, which are accountable to, and often nominated directly by, central government rather than a directly-elected agency;

- regulation via contract and/or performance criteria.

This approach has had some positive effects on providers. Most obviously, often fierce competition has encouraged most colleges to attempt to promote their offerings more vigorously and widely, and to improve the accessibility of provision and the flexibility of courses. However, the dysfunctions of the quasi-market in tertiary provision have been well documented (Kennedy, 1997; Scott, 1995; Spours & Lucas, 1996). They include:

- the loss of strategic oversight and quality control of provision, expressed in the duplication of low-cost, paper-based and high volume courses, a bias against expensive or minority programmes, and often uncontrolled or incoherent expansion;

- excessive competition between providers to recruit learners, often resulting in placements on inappropriate courses;

- a democratic deficit, expressed in a lack of formal accountability to local and regional communities, and manifest at its worst in sleaze and abuse of public funds;

- excessive bureaucracy and regulatory red tape consequent upon both the sheer complexity of funding enormously diverse learning activities across the country, and the need to exercise audit control in disparate contexts;

- hierarchical differentiation between providers and the distribution of learners across them.

Careers education, advice and guidance

The structural changes described above have had two major implications for the Careers Service. First, the development of a quasi-market in tertiary provision has placed great pressure on the Careers Service to ensure that students receive some measure of disinterested advice and guidance. Young people must now assess a complex array of opportunities in the 'learning marketplace'. There is a tendency for providers, driven by funding imperatives, to recruit or retain students on the basis of institutional need rather than educational judgement. In this context, student choice is a chimera in the absence of effective and impartial advice and guidance.

Second, the absence of strategic oversight has meant that it falls to the Careers Service to ensure that disadvantaged or disengaged young people do not slip through the complex net of provision. These are two considerable burdens to have placed on agencies which were themselves subject to organisational upheaval in the 1990s and in whom trust has not always been forthcoming from either clients or partners. Careers Services are themselves delivered under contract following their removal from LEAs. As we noted in Chapter 4, there is evidence that this has led, in some areas, to a lack of focus on critical issues.

The 1997 Education Act attempted to mitigate 'provider-capture' of potential students by introducing new requirements for schools to offer careers education programmes in Years 9-11, and obligations for schools and colleges to ensure that students have access to impartial careers advice. Whilst valuable in themselves, these reforms were premised on the need for an honest broker in an 'ersatz' market.

But in addition to the dysfunctions of this market which we have noted above, the concept of a tertiary system driven solely by individual 'consumer choice' is inherently flawed. First, it ignores the role which other stakeholders – principally local employers and the local community – have in designing and steering the system. If the input of these stakeholders is mediated solely through the choices of students, then tertiary provision could develop in ways which manifestly fail to meet the needs of the local labour market or respond to the interests of the community as a whole. Second, it skews the role of careers education and guidance to a market-making function, and downgrades its place within the curriculum.

Those who are furthest removed from participation in education and training are the least likely to be served by a Careers Service redesigned as an honest broker in a tertiary learning market. Yet the Careers Service has the potential to be a key bridging agency, assisting young people, particularly the vulnerable, through periods of transition. The reorientation of the Careers Service towards these young people is likely to require a co-operative environment in which institutions and agencies work together to raise levels of participation and achievement.

Recent and planned reforms

In order to lift participation and raise achievement in tertiary education, there needs to be reform of the existing institutional framework. The current framework serves the needs of the lowest attainers badly: it is fragmented and competitive, when action to raise achievement requires coherence and co-operation, as well as a rigorous client focus. Nor is it likely to be able to support the development of a more flexible curriculum and qualifications system for 14-19 year olds. Institutional divisions inhibit the sharing of resources and collaboration over provision at a local level.

The recent government reform agenda can best be described as increased co-operation within the status quo. Some collaboration and strategic oversight of further education and training has already taken place, encouraged by modest sums of government funds, such as the FEFC Collaboration Fund, to promote such development. Likewise, sub-regional partnerships and local fora have been convened to establish progress towards the National Targets for Education and Training and to submit funding bids for specific projects. Yet until recently co-operation has been ad hoc and marginal to the largely competitive environment.

New reform agendas are intended to take the worst edges off this situation without fundamentally re-drawing institutional boundaries.

These include:

- the widening participation partnerships generated in further education as a consequence of the Kennedy Report;

- further efforts to merge or rationalise further education provision;

- the New Start projects for disaffected and disengaged young people;

- the recent Green Paper for England on lifelong learning *The Learning Age* which signals greater collaboration and strategic oversight of tertiary provision, including new planning arrangements to be published in the near future.

A number of modifications to the current structure of tertiary provision could be developed, building on existing trends in collaborative work. Planned and potential measures include:

- requiring all key partners in a locality to draw up a strategic development plan, detailing mechanisms for co-operation in pursuit of education and training targets;

- broadening the size and scope of funds for collaboration and widening participation, perhaps by top-slicing from the FEFC budget. Allocation would be determined, as now, by regional and sub-regional groupings, inclusive of LEA membership;

- carrying forward reform of college governing bodies and TEC boards to ensure greater accountability to local communities and more effective liaison with LEAs, whilst guaranteeing a reciprocal right of representation to colleges on the local authority education committee (although we should note that accountability is not just about elected representatives but the integral relationship of a college to its students and community);

- further harmonising inspection arrangements, including joint working between OFSTED, the FEFC inspectorate and the Training Standards Council;

- formalising franchised provision of further education in school sixth-forms by legislating to allow the FEFC to fund such work directly where it takes place within agreed partnerships, as will be the case in Wales.

These proposals leave the basic division of responsibilities in tertiary provision untouched. Nonetheless, they remove the worst features of competition and promote greater openness and consistency in provision. They have the merit of securing sensible change without imposing costly structural upheaval.

The regionalisation agenda

It has been argued in this and other chapters that measures to tackle non-participation and disaffection are much more likely to be effective if there is improved co-ordination and co-operation between the various agencies with responsibility for tertiary provision. As we have seen, this is now beginning to take place. In the long-term, however, policy-makers may wish to undertake more fundamental structural reform of tertiary education and training, particularly if co-operation within the status quo does not prove sufficient to address the dysfunctions outlined previously. What, hypothetically, might such reform entail, recognising that organisational change is complex, demanding and often contentious?

In this respect, the potential for regionally-based reform of tertiary provision is promising. With the creation of Regional Development Agencies (RDAs) and the prospect of emerging regional government, even if at a modest and uneven pace, the regional tier will become increasingly important to the delivery of post-16 education and training. The FEFC already has regional committees and TECs draw their funding from regional government offices. In anticipation of further regional development, the evolution of tertiary provision could take an increasingly regional shape, building where possible on existing structures. A number of different options are available for regionalisation of tertiary provision.

Strengthening regional oversight and planning of the existing system

Previous discussion of regional development of tertiary education has focused on the creation of regional planning and co-ordination bodies to oversee the patchwork of local provision (Scott, 1995; Spours & Lucas, 1996). The key providers and agencies in tertiary education – LEAs, TECs and colleges – would submit development plans to a regional planning body for negotiation and approval within an overall regional strategy. The FEFC's statutory responsibility for ensuring the adequacy and sufficiency of further education provision for 16-19 year olds would pass to the regional body, although the Council would continue to fund colleges against their strategic plans. The regional tier would provide a framework within which stronger institutional partnerships – between schools, colleges, TECs and universities – could evolve. The representation of all the key stakeholders in tertiary provision within the regional agency, including LEAs, would also go some way to tackling the democratic deficit.

It has previously been suggested that revamped and democratised regional committees of the FEFC could become the new regional bodies (Scott, 1995; Spours & Lucas, 1996). However, the creation of the Regional Development Agencies (RDAs) has added a new dimension to the institutional landscape. Under existing plans, the role of RDAs in education and training will be limited to assessing the contribution of TECs towards regional objectives and engaging further and higher education fully in the regional agenda. The RDAs will seek to contribute to the work of further and higher education institutions and improve co-operation between the sectors. However, the creation of RDAs offers much greater reform potential.

A stronger role for Regional Development Agencies

How could the role of the RDAs be strengthened? In the first place, TECs should be funded directly by RDAs and made accountable to them. This would ensure greater co-ordination of activity. RDAs would be well-placed to control the regional training budget, determine regional skills strategies and contract with TECs. More radically, TECs could be absorbed as wholly-owned subsidiaries of the RDAs.

What would this mean for tertiary education? With TECs under the ownership of RDAs, the potential for co-ordination of strategy and funding between training and further education would be extensive. Funding norms could be brought into convergence, either through greater flexibility in FEFC allocations, or through a direct extension of FEFC funding norms to TEC provision for young people (See Chapter 7).

Secondly, and in parallel to this enhanced role for RDAs, the FEFC's regional committees could be revamped and strengthened. The FEFC could devolve a proportion of its global funding for colleges to its regional committees, for allocation after negotiation with the RDAs. Alternatively, a new dedicated funding stream could be created, on the basis of an expansion of the existing collaboration fund, for dispersion through the regional committees, again after negotiation with the RDAs. The primary objective of this new role for the regional committees would be to provide the necessary forum for planning and foresight of tertiary education, backed up by real funding. This strategic foresight would be co-ordinated with regional training strategies through liaison with the RDAs.

To be effective, however, the FEFC regional committees would need to be democratised and broadened – as previously envisaged – so as to include LEA representation. On this basis, the committees would have the authority to share planning oversight – necessarily with a light touch – of all local tertiary provision, including school sixth-forms. The committees, like the RDAs, would receive local strategic plans for consideration within overall determination of the regional strategy for tertiary education and training. Once the regional strategy had been finalised, funding allocations from the pool of regional resources could be determined.

In this scenario, there is parallel development of the strategic capacity of RDAs and new forums for regionalisation of tertiary education. This is to ensure that two broad objectives can be met: first, that there is a viable mechanism for co-ordination of tertiary provision in schools and colleges; and second, that tertiary provision in its broadest sense – including TEC-funded activity – can be developed at a regional level. It is vital, however, that regional bureaucracies are not reinvented. The self-governing status of providers should be respected, in order to retain the benefits of flexibility and innovation. Planning should be as light as is necessary to ensure that broad objectives are met. It should provide a framework in which local co-operation can flourish.

A powerful role for regional government

As regional government develops – from regional chambers to regional assemblies – the education and training functions of the RDAs are increasingly likely to pass over to regional government. Likewise, regional government could assume the functions of the regional committees of the FEFC. In the long-term, tertiary education and training could come under the umbrella of regional government.

Conclusion

The regional government scenario is a long-term one. In the short term, it is likely that funding responsibilities for tertiary education will remain split between local authorities, further education colleges and TECs. Consequently, the potential for better co-ordination and transparency is likely to be sought, as it has been in the past, at the level of resource allocation as much as in institutional partnership. In the next chapter, more radical ideas for the unification of funding arrangements are examined.

Chapter 7: Funding learning

The funding of education and training is relevant to disaffection and non-participation for two reasons. First, the funding system as a whole, and the methods employed by the various bodies responsible for education and training, have a major impact on the focus and behaviour of education institutions and other organisations providing for young people. Second, the funding available for the young people themselves is a key influence on their own decisions about education and training activity.

This chapter examines the various means by which employers and the state fund education and training, both as regards institutions and individuals. It looks at how funding principles affect the disadvantaged and concludes with examination of the idea of a single post-16 funding council.

Support for young people

Financial support for young people in the 16-19 age group is an area currently subject to central government review, including as part of the proposed reform of discretionary awards. The Education and Employment Select Committee has also recently examined this area of policy (1998a). It clearly has significant implications for non-participating and disaffected young people.

The current state of play

The following are the main forms of support available to young people and their families:

- Child Benefit is payable to parents up to the 19th birthday of the young person if he or she is in full-time education. It counts as income for those parents in receipt of Income Support or Job-Seekers Allowance and is deducted in full from entitlements. Young people count as dependants for Family Credit purposes only if they are in relevant full-time education.

- Allowances are paid to those on Youth Training and may be topped-up by TECs or employers. Bridging Allowances are available to those who have left jobs or YT places.

- Income Support is paid to young people only if they fall into exceptional categories, such as single parents, carers, and those with disabilities.

- Job-Seekers Allowance (JSA) is available to prescribed groups of young people, such as care leavers and those living away from home. JSA can also be paid on a discretionary basis for those likely to suffer severe hardship.

- Educational Maintenance Allowances are paid by local authorities at their discretion, usually on the basis of a means test.

As is clear from this list, young people in general have no entitlement to social security benefits. Instead, since 1988, when this entitlement was withdrawn, they have been given the 'guarantee' of a training place. As we have noted, however, TECs have struggled to supply the necessary places to meet this guarantee. This has undoubtedly meant real hardship for young people who experience 'Status Zero'. Of the 82,000 16-17 year olds unemployed but not in full-time education in Autumn 1997, only 23 per cent were in receipt of income from the state in the form of Jobseeker's Allowance (mainly under the severe hardship provision) and Bridging Allowance (Labour Force Survey; Chatrik and Convery, 1998).

At the same time, the level of the allowance for those on Youth Training is considered abysmal by young people. It contributes to the image of Youth Training as low status, slave labour. In part, however, this is because many Youth Training places are not viewed as genuine traineeships: young people who are not trained properly and who do not have the prospect of employment at the end of a placement are less likely to accept low allowances as the price to pay of an apprenticeship period.

Key problems to tackle

In terms of the various forms of support available for young people, there are at least five major problems that policy-makers need to address.

1. Substantial numbers of young people are living in poverty and/or are homeless either because they are not entitled to benefits, or because the benefits to which they are entitled are inadequate or difficult to access.

2.   There are far too many anomalies in the system, with different types of young people being treated differently for no apparent reason. For example, poorer young people who stay on in school get free school meals and clothing allowances, while those at colleges do not. There is also substantial misdirection and inefficient distribution of resources, the best known example being the payment of Child Benefit to parents of young people between the ages of 16 and 19 only if they are in full-time education and regardless of parental income.

3.   Systems of support do not give enough incentives for young people to stay in education and training, to learn and achieve, particularly at sub-degree level.

4.   Existing systems of support fail adequately to reflect the complexity and flexibility of the youth labour market and are based on outdated distinctions of activity. Individual young people engage in various combinations of full-time and part-time work, full-time and part-time study, other activities and unemployment (as discussed in Chapter 3). They also move between combinations of activity, often quite frequently.

5.   The system as a whole is unnecessarily confusing and complex for young people. There are far too many barriers to young people becoming aware of the opportunities and forms of support that are available to them, and understanding what their rights and entitlements are (a 150 page book [Maclagan, 1997] is necessary to set these out).

A single allowance?

It is clear that at some point there should be a fundamental re-examination of the whole field of financial support for young people. One possible way forward would be the consolidation of the various forms of support that have been described into a single allowance, along the lines of the Youth Allowance currently being introduced in Australia. The Youth Allowance is an income support payment to young people, including students and those looking for work, replacing a range of existing payments.

In this country a single allowance could cover the 16-19 age range or could even be extended to people in their twenties as well. The simplified allowance might replace all of the allowances currently provided to young people or their families, including Youth Training, Educational Maintenance Allowances, Income Support and Job-Seekers Allowance for certain groups, and Child Benefit for the parents of those aged between 16 and 19 in full-time education.

If such a system were to be introduced it would almost certainly require means-testing of parents and would entail some 'deadweight' costs. Parents are already subject to means-testing if and when their children enter higher education. A single allowance, means-tested at 16, should be designed to articulate smoothly with arrangements for higher education support.

A single allowance should be based on a number of key principles. It should:

- be simple, transparent and readily accessible;

- provide incentives for participation and achievement, and require evidence that these were taking place;

- recognise and respond flexibly to the different circumstances of young people, for example their living arrangements;

- prioritise support for those young people and their families who most need it;

- ensure a basic standard of living for all young people;

- respond to changes in the labour market by taking account of the full range of learning and employment activities available for young people.

The idea of a single allowance is put forward here simply to provoke discussion. It also dovetails with other proposals in this document that aim to improve co-ordination of policy and services for young people. To draw up a workable blueprint for a single allowance would be a substantial exercise. However, there can be no doubt that simplification of the system of support for young people, and effective co-ordination of policy-making, should be a major concern for government and its partners.

The responsibility of employers

For young people in work, particularly 16 and 17 year olds, the question of who is responsible for ensuring they get training, and who pays for it, is a key policy area.

Current policy

Earlier, in Chapter 5, we discussed the work-based route and reforms to that route and some of the problems that have arisen relating to qualifications. As was mentioned, recent government legislation will give 16 and 17 year olds in work who are not in full-time secondary or further education, and have not reached NVQ level 2, an entitlement to the equivalent of day release to study towards an approved qualification.

This policy is a long overdue and welcome step forward. However, we should be aware that employers of 16 and 17 year olds will not be compelled to provide education and training (whether in-house or with an external provider) to those who have not reached level 2. The new legislation provides an entitlement to study to the individual but does not impose a duty on the employer to ensure that training and education takes place. By locating responsibility with the individual for exercising their right to study, it is likely many young people will not receive training, either because they do not understand their rights or because they do not avail themselves of recourse to an employment tribunal if the employer refuses to release them. Indeed, many of these young people will be the least likely to take up their rights. An additional problem arises in that those who lack level 2 qualifications will be unattractive to employers unless the obligation to train is extended to all young people in full-time jobs.

Future policy

One policy worth considering is the extension of traineeships across the full-time youth labour market. All young people employed full-time would be employed on mandatory traineeships. This proposal has been put forward in the recent past by the Commission on Public Policy and British Business (1997). Employers would be compensated for the costs of training and day release in order to balance the new obligations. At the same time, trainees would remain exempt from the forthcoming national minimum wage, as recommended by the Low Pay Commission and accepted by the Government. Such an approach would ensure that employers continued to take on young people and did not substitute older workers into their jobs.

A different approach would be to extend the government's New Deal to cover the 16-19 age group, with a more limited qualifying period than six months for entry to the programme, as proposed by the Education and Employment Select Committee (1998), which raised concerns about the New Deal subsidy displacing unemployment from 18-24 year olds to 16 and 17 year olds. Properly reconstructed, 16-18 year olds could be offered New Deal options, in addition to National Traineeships and Modern Apprenticeships, rather than the current training place guarantee, supported by an allowance and extended over two years. This could be achieved on the basis of a merger of the New Start and New Deal programmes.

The rationale for this is obvious: it is largely the same client group at different ages which is being dealt with by both programmes. It would be sensible therefore to invest resources in young people at an earlier age, rather than wait for them to become eligible for the New Deal at 18. It is, after all, possible to identify at 14 or even younger who is most likely to require such an intervention. This approach would have the additional advantage of preventing any displacement of employer investment in Youth Training/National Traineeships by government New Deal subsidies for the older age group. There are complex issues to be resolved here which are beyond the scope of this paper. Nonetheless, they are worthy of further exploration.

Existing institutional funding arrangements

What then of the major resource allocation mechanisms for tertiary education and training? Unsurprisingly, the divisions between learning routes and institutional environments are paralleled in the funding of 16-19 education and training:

- local authorities provide funding for school sixth forms according to the Local Management of Schools formula;[11]

- the Further Education Funding Council funds learners in further education, tertiary and sixth-form colleges;

- Training and Enterprise Councils fund Youth Training/National Traineeships and Modern Apprenticeships.

Differences in these funding systems have been reflected in variations in the level of resources received by providers, both within and between different sectors. Criticisms of complexity and inequity have been commonplace. In addition, the different funding systems all have internal strengths and weaknesses:

School sixth-form funding

There are very few people in the country who fully understand the extraordinary complexities of local government funding. In fact, the funding of students in school sixth-forms is relatively straightforward. LEAs allocate funding for schools according to the Local Management of Schools formula. At least 80 per cent of the funds delegated to schools must be based on pupils numbers via Age Weighted Pupil Units (AWPUs). In general terms, sixth-form AWPUs are higher than those for pupils in compulsory education.

School sixth-form funding is also straightforward and simple in comparison to the other main post-16 funding systems. Yet this virtue is also a vice. Unlike colleges or training providers, schools do not have any output-related funding incentives to ensure that students are retained on courses or achieve their qualification aims. Whilst LEAs may claw back resources for students who do not stay on the school-roll, the funding levers are not as powerful as in other forms of provision.

However, schools do have input-related financial incentives to recruit their existing students into their sixth-forms and this has led to the accusations noted earlier that careers advice and guidance to Year 11 pupils has been biased by institutional self-interest. Moreover, schools have been able to subsidise uneconomic and narrow sixth-form provision from funding for compulsory age pupils, allowing them an unjustified advantage over neighbouring institutions.

Further education sector funding

The basic principles of FEFC funding – that funding for learners should be based on units, determined by a tariff, for some combination of the costs of recruitment, retention and achievement – are widely accepted. When it was introduced, the new 'methodology' was seen by many as an advance over funding determined on the basis of full-time equivalents, since the latter provided no incentive to ensure that students stayed on courses and achieved results, and was biased against part-time learning. The FEFC methodology is largely neutral between modes of learning; it is transparent; it provides incentives to recruit, retain and push students towards achievement; and it has additional support built in for the unemployed, those with learning difficulties and/or disabilities, and to a very limited extent for those needing child care.

At the same time, the FEFC approach has been criticised on a number of fronts:

● its complexity requires significant administrative effort from colleges;

● it has a tendency to drive the curriculum, rather than vice versa;

● throughout colleges there has been a reduction in taught hours for full-time students;

● cost differentials between courses which are capital intensive and those which are paper-based are not reflected adequately, which has led to the loss of some strategically important but expensive forms of provision such as engineering;

● it provides little scope for curriculum innovation or enrichment, particularly for the 16-18 age group;

● it has until now given only limited recognition to the differential costs of providing learning in areas of social disadvantage.

As a result of the recommendations of the Kennedy Report, the funding methodology is to be reformed in this last key respect. The FEFC will introduce a widening participation factor to the funding tariff from 1998/9, based on the deprivation index used by the Department of the Environment, Transport and the Regions. Students from deprived backgrounds, identified on the basis of postcodes, will attract increased resources. The principal problem with this approach is that focusing funding by area rather than targeting individuals assumes that disadvantage is concentrated in particular areas. Such an approach is likely to benefit many individuals who do not need support, and to miss many that do.

In respect of disaffected and disadvantaged students, there is a further issue which requires consideration, and that is the fact that the FEFC does not have the legal power to fund provision for 14-16 year olds on Bridge or Link courses. The status of these courses is unclear but, by and large, colleges are reimbursed for their costs by LEAs. The funding and legal status of this valuable form of provision needs clarification.

TEC funding

TECs do not have to replicate exactly the way they are funded by the DfEE in the contracts they negotiate with training providers. They can attract additional resources provided by employers but this is not realistic for the cohort of young people that are disadvantaged or disaffected. Generally TECs have followed the broad parameters established by central government. Over recent years, this has been based on different combinations of funding for starts and outcomes achieved. In 1997/8 TECs were funded to move more broadly in line with FEFC funding – that is, on the basis of starts, numbers in training and outcomes.

The output related funding element of TEC funding is significantly higher than it is for colleges – some 30 per cent compared to 8 per cent. For those providers – particularly in the voluntary sector – who have contracted with TECs to deliver training for lower attainers, the experience of output related funding has not been successful. It can be argued that a measure of output related funding can push providers to focus on attainment. However, extensive reliance on payment by results leads to well-attested problems:

● it can lead providers to 'cherry-pick', avoiding recruitment of those least likely to achieve or those who may take longer to achieve, including those with low levels of basic skills, those with special educational needs, the homeless, and those in care;

● it favours cheaper fast-track courses rather than those which have more relevance to the labour market;

● it can encourage providers to dampen students' expectations and place them on lower level courses than their potential merits;

● it can lead to lower standards if the provider has any responsibility for assessment.

In short, the TEC funding regime creates substantial disincentives to meet the needs of the disadvantaged and the disaffected because of the exposure to risk of financial non-viability through failure to recover costs.

Complexities and inequities

In the wider tertiary context, it is the complexity and inequity which different resource allocation mechanisms give rise to which has exercised policy-makers in recent years. As the Kennedy Report noted:

> Each of the funding routes has been developed for separate policy objectives. We found that the bewildering variety of complex systems, the interaction between them and the plethora of specific and challenge funding presented real problems. Such funding arrangements inhibit informed debate and absorb disproportionate costs and management time. (Kennedy, 1997: 47)

Partly in response to such concerns, the previous Conservative administration spent considerable effort investigating the possibility of convergence in funding norms and allocation levels. From the then government's perspective, a level playing field was not just about addressing providers' disquiet. It was also seen as important in opening the way to the logical outcome of a free market tertiary system: customer controlled resource allocation, in which the student would purchase provision directly from a supplier, whether it be school sixth-form, training provider or college.

In the event, the system of credits for government-supported training that was introduced by the Conservative government – Training Credits – was aimed at the poorly-resourced and low status end of provision. Trying to establish a workable unit for a learning credit – whether cash or entitlement-based – across all forms of education and training for 16 to 19 year olds appeared to prove beyond the limits of practical or political feasibility. Although learning credits for 16-19 year olds are no longer on the political agenda, issues of equity, consistency and simplicity in the funding of tertiary provision have yet to be resolved. These are complex issues which have significant practical and political implications. They are intimately bound up with the institutional framework of tertiary provision.

Funding principles, under-achievement and disaffection

At the level of principle, there is consensus that funding should be curriculum-led and equitably distributed. There is no a priori reason why the unit of resource should vary according to the type of institution. However, it is now accepted that the higher costs of educating those with low prior educational attainment in areas of social disadvantage should be recognised in funding allocations.

To return to first principles, it is worth restating the case for and against different types of funding made by the Further Education Funding Council in its consultative document, *Funding Learning* (FEFC, 1992):

- *Funding enrolments*

  The advantages of funding on the basis of enrolments are simplicity and broad relation of resources to student numbers. It promotes expansion of provision. The disadvantages are that resources are allocated regardless of whether students complete programmes or achieve qualifications; that expansion can take precedence over quality; and that it is inequitable to part-time learning.

- *Student achievements*

  As we have seen, payment by results is superficially attractive because it focuses funding on the primary objective of learning – achievement. The disadvantages are that in the absence of a 'value added' approach providers are tempted to exclude those who are least likely to achieve and may lower their standards if they have any responsibility for final assessment.

- *Funding the different elements of learning*

  If funding based on entry or exit is problematic, then it seems sensible to align it to the costs of all the different elements of the learning – entry, on-programme, and exit – which is what the FEFC chose to do. The important issue is then to decide the balance between the different elements. Ideally, the balance should reflect the actual costs of provision, with a small output-related element to retain the focus on achievement. The advantages of such a system are that it gives providers incentives to offer high-quality initial advice and guidance; it can meet the on-programme costs of learning with reasonable frequency; and it can provide an incentive to ensure achievement without distorting recruitment patterns.

At the level of principle, therefore, an equitable system of funding tertiary education across different institutions should be based on the three elements of the FEFC approach. Difficult questions arise, however, on the basis for implementation. For example:

- can the problems identified with FEFC funding – such as its administrative cost – be overcome?

- is the problem of separate pre- and post-16 funding systems for schools insurmountable?

- can FEFC funding cope with unitisation of the curriculum?

A single post-16 funding council?

One way forward for tertiary education which has attracted support is the creation of a single funding council for post-16 education and training. Three variants of this proposal may be identified, depending on the prospective partners to the merger:

1.   A Tertiary Education Funding Council: adding school sixth-forms to the FEFC.

2.   An Education and Training Funding Council: passing TEC funding for 16-19 year olds to the FEFC (and possibly school sixth-forms).

3.   Education, Training and Enterprise Councils: extending the role of TECs (or LEAs) also to purchase college (and possibly school sixth-form) provision for 16-19 year olds.

Each of these variants is now examined.

Variant 1: Tertiary Education Funding Council

The first variant is that local education authorities would surrender the funding of school sixth-forms to the FEFC which would provide resources to schools on the basis of its funding methodology. This would create a larger body, in effect a Tertiary Education Funding Council. This has a number of advantages. First, it would ensure that all public providers of tertiary education were funded on an equitable basis according to the same principles. Equity and transparency would have been achieved. Second, depending on the strictness of rule enforcement, schools would be less able to cross subsidise uneconomic sixth-forms offering narrow curricula. Nor would they be able to open small sixth-forms in defiance of regulations, as hitherto they have done, to the detriment of other local institutions. Third, a basic structural divide in tertiary education between local authority and FEFC provision would have been overcome. This would open the way to greater co-operation between different providers.

However, there are significant disadvantages to this proposal (Scott, 1995). The most obvious is that school funding would be split between pre- and post-16 provision (although it is worth noting that further education colleges already have at least three major funding sources). This could create significant difficulties for school planning and would lead to a rise, at least in the short-term, in administrative costs. The biggest administrative headaches would be suffered in areas with predominantly 11-18 schools. This argument is not as strong as it might first seem. More seriously, the Tertiary Education Funding Council model would result in an even more extensive democratic deficit in post-compulsory provision, as further parts of the system passed under the sway of the FEFC. Finally, there could be an impact on post-16 participation rates, as transitions would be interrupted.

Variant 2: Education and Training Funding Council

The second variant would be to rationalise provision by combining TEC and FEFC funding for 16-19 provision by passing TEC funding for the age group to the FEFC. The enhanced FEFC – in effect an Education and Training Funding Council – would fund those on training places as well as off-the-job training for young employees. An extension of this variant is to combine it with Variant 1 and include the funding of school sixth-forms as well.

The strategy of passing TEC funding to the FEFC also has problems. The most critical is the loss of an agency which can negotiate locally with employers and the voluntary sector for the delivery of training places. Unless traineeships are mandatory for all young people, or the

Employment Service provides a brokerage function as it does under the New Deal, then some such local agency is necessary. It is unclear whether colleges could fulfil the role themselves simply on the basis of employer representation on the governing bodies of colleges and on the regional committees of the FEFC itself.

Variant 3: Education, Training and Enterprise Councils

In this variant, TECs are broadened to become funders not only of Youth Training/National Traineeships and Modern Apprenticeships, but of the rest of college provision for the 16-19 age group. The FEFC would be reduced to funding learning for those aged over 19. This would set up a purchaser/provider split at the local level, which could conceivably also embrace school sixth-forms.

The drawback of this variant is that colleges would have to negotiate a greater number of contracts with the new councils whilst still remaining funded by the FEFC for the bulk of their work. This would increase the burden of red tape to which they are already subject. It is not clear that the gains would be significant, other than to rationalise part of the funding for the age group.

The new councils would become powerful players in tertiary education, and there would be further problems if they were spawned from TECs. The accountability of TECs to the local community is limited and they have a troubled track record in the delivery of the training guarantee for young people. An alternative of this variant would be to extend the role of LEAs to purchase all 16-19 provision. This alternative is not only unimaginable for political reasons, but is also possibly unfeasible since LEAs could never be neutral as purchasers. However, the idea has some similarities to the proposals put forward by the National Commission on Education (1993) for the development of Education and Training Boards to fund schools and training programmes for youth and the unemployed (although the NCE did not suggest that these boards would fund further education colleges).

Conclusion

Each of the above options discusses reform as a set of shifts between existing institutional bodies. However, the previous chapter examined how the institutional landscape might change with the development of a regional agenda. Consequently, it is possible to think of the above options as, in different ways, potential elements of a regional reform package. However they are configured, and however they relate to RDAs, such single funding councils might be established in each region, as a prelude to the development of regional government. Alternatively, reform of resource allocation could focus purely on funding mechanisms, regardless of changes to the distribution of responsibilities between local, regional and national bodies. In the final analysis, these judgements cannot be made *a priori*, but only of the basis of experience and political consideration.

Chapter 8: Conclusions

The problem of under-achievement, disaffection and social exclusion

Educational attainment is critical to the success of individuals, companies and society as a whole. Skills and knowledge are increasingly fundamental to participation in the labour market and in wider civil society. Those who lack skills or suffer low levels of educational attainment are becoming more and more vulnerable to social exclusion and labour market marginalisation. People with basic skills problems are particularly at risk.

Consequently, we cannot afford to ignore anybody in the drive to raise standards of achievement. Yet there are large numbers of young people (between one in ten and one in twelve) – often, but not always, the same individuals – who regularly truant, who leave school without any qualifications, and who then do not go into education, training or employment. Amongst these are a smaller number of young people who are temporarily or permanently excluded from schools. As general attainment levels rise, not just in Britain but in almost every country, these groups are being left further behind.

The significant numbers of young people who for various reasons become disengaged from the education system are an ongoing problem, which successive governments have failed to tackle. Yet while certain groups of young people face multiple disadvantage, there is no evidence for the emergence of a *discrete* youth underclass suffering from under-achievement, disaffection and social exclusion. Changes in advanced societies have certainly transformed the youth labour market and educational participation. But they have not created – nor do they seem set to create – a wholly distinct and deprived group of young people. Many young people move in and out of different categories of activity (like full-time and part-time education and work, and unemployment) through complex pathways during their late teens. It is therefore dangerous to assume that there is a youth underclass defined by structural or behavioural factors.

The stereotype of disaffected youth also tends to be male, and this is reflected in the much greater attention given to boys than girls in this area by the media and policy-makers. At one level this is justified: it is mainly boys who are excluded from school and, ultimately, crime is much more likely to be committed by young males than young females. However, in educational terms, under-achievement and disaffection are not particularly male problems. Gender differences are negligible at the low end of achievement, in regular truancy, and in non-participation in education, training or employment by the age of 17.

Factors other than gender appear to be much more important in explaining disaffection and underachievement. Most importantly, there are strong associations with social and family background, and with previous educational attainment (including the acquisition of basic skills). Furthermore, it is quite clear that certain groups of young people do suffer forms of social and educational exclusion. Those in care, the young homeless, those with special needs, certain ethnic minorities and others, experience significant disadvantage, albeit with specific causes and consequences.

Disaffection is also notably caused by boredom with the environment of school, by bullying, and by the effects of peer group pressures. These are issues we have addressed in this report. We have done so on the basis of a policy approach that is inclusive and addresses the needs of all young people, whatever their level of achievement, and whatever their pathways across categories of education, employment and other activities.

To put our conclusions into context, what we know from the statistical and survey evidence available to us is the following:

- the proportion of young people at the lowest attainment levels is high, and the gap between the lowest and average/higher attainers is widening;

- numbers of regular truants, possibly the best measure of pure disaffection that we have, are fairly stable and may even have fallen, but there remains a significant hard-core of persistent truants;

- rates of exclusion from school have risen sharply in recent years (although they may have now flattened), but this has been due more to institutional behaviour than any increase in disaffection and disruptive behaviour;

- the proportion of young people not participating in education, training or employment after leaving school (the so-called 'Status Zero' group) has fluctuated, and the research evidence shows that young people tend to move in and out of this category; at the same time, the numbers are far too large in particular geographical areas and amongst certain ethnic groups; and in general terms, they are unsustainable in the context of rising demands for the skills needed for work and active citizenship;

- full-time participation in post-16 education has peaked and fallen back in recent years, whilst achievements gained through training by those who go into work after leaving school remain poor.

Key issues for policy-makers

Our starting point in this book has been that high standards are for everyone. This does not mean diluting standards so that anyone can reach them. It means creating a system in which barriers to achieving those high standards are wherever possible removed. A system in which a 'gold standard' is preserved for an elite, and in which there is tolerance of large numbers of young people not participating or failing to achieve anything, is incompatible with the demands of the economy as we move into the 21st century. We therefore welcome the renewed attention that the Government is giving to those at the lowest levels of attainment. We particularly welcome the recommendations of the report of the Social Exclusion Unit on truancy and exclusion.

In this report we have covered policies for the whole 14–19 age range. We believe that the problem of under-achievement and non-participation is partly caused by the sharp break at 16 that occurs in qualifications and in organisational and funding arrangements. Performance at GCSE is the key determinant of post-16 activity, effectively sorting young people into fairly rigid tracks of academic, general vocational and work-based routes. It is also the best predictor of entry into the so-called 'Status Zero' group who fall through the gaps and do not participate in any form of education, training or employment at all.

Overlaying the problems caused by the three-track qualifications system are further difficulties caused by systems of organisation and funding that are highly complex and confusing. These systems also encourage often dysfunctional competition for students, and embody a number of inequalities between similar provision provided in different contexts. The organisational system faced by young people is cluttered by intermediaries. In education and training alone there are TECs, LEAs, FEFC (national, regional and colleges themselves), Employment Service, competing awarding bodies and examining boards, government offices and soon Regional Development Agencies. These organisations themselves, alone or in partnerships, spend huge amounts of time and energy bidding for resources from central government, from challenge funds and from Europe. It is hard to see how such a system could not engender bureaucratic waste. Meanwhile, outside of the formal education and training system, disaffected and vulnerable young people (particularly those in care) often receive fragmented and confusing services from different departments within local government.

In short, the system for organising and funding post-compulsory education and training as a whole is irrational and sub-optimal. If it were to be designed from scratch it would not look anything like this. We therefore argue in this report that in the long-term some organisational reform will be necessary.

A key problem for the disadvantaged and disaffected is the disincentives to target them or meet their needs that are now built into systems, most notably the interaction of performance measures and funding arrangements. In schools, the concentration in the recent past of league tables (and in particular the way that the media report them) on the 5 A* to C benchmark within the context of pupil-led funding formulae encourages schools to concentrate their efforts on pupils around and just below this level, and to neglect under-achievers. Similarly, TECs, whose league tables take no account taken of the educational level or socio-economic background of the young people they serve, also have little incentive to meet the needs of the disadvantaged, particularly since 30 per cent of funding is output-related.

A key theme which emerges from this report is that only a minority of young people follow simple employment and learning pathways when they leave post-compulsory education. It is very common for young people to combine and move between different activities, often several times: full-time and part-time education or training, employment, unemployment and voluntary work. Sometimes the changes they make are their own choices (or they are actively encouraged to make them by the various competing agencies); at other times changes are imposed by circumstances. Individuals have complex needs, in terms of qualifications, locations for education and training, work experience and impartial advice and guidance. Existing qualifications, organisation and funding systems are not nearly flexible enough.

Another key theme is the need to address disaffection in the context of whole families. A substantial body of research show that family background, and in particular parental education, have a major impact on achievement and attitudes to education:

- there is a strong intergenerational effect in basic skills, in which there is a high correlation between low levels amongst parents and their children, such that young people who most need help at home are the least likely to get it;

- children of lone parents are educationally disadvantaged and the particular needs of teenage lone parents themselves do not receive nearly enough attention;

- there is evidence that a significant proportion of truancy is condoned, for various reasons, by parents.

Policy geared towards raising achievement and tackling social exclusion needs therefore to look beyond individual young people themselves. Key initiatives like New Start, Education Action Zones and even New Deal should aim to play a role in family support (for example family literacy schemes). Young people in care face particular problems. Local authorities do not perform their role as corporate parents in anything like a satisfactory way, at least as far education is concerned.

Finally, we identify in this report the need for a more preventative approach to under-achievement and disaffection including the development of robust systems for tracking disaffection as early as possible and more integrated ways of dealing with disaffected pupils in schools.

Policy recommendations

The policies aimed at raising achievement and tackling social exclusion that we discuss in the report fall into three main categories:

- current government policies;

- short- to medium-term policies that we recommend prior to wider structural reform of education and training;

- a long-term policy agenda that we recommend for consideration.

In conclusion we will draw together and summarise policies under these headings.

Current government policies

The Government has put in place a wide range of initiatives which aim to tackle under-achievement, disaffection and social exclusion which are mentioned throughout this report. These are the responsibility of many different parts of the Department for Education and Employment and of other bodies outside. We list the major ones below:

- Behaviour Support Plans (see page 45);

- written home/school agreements (p 47);

- Social Exclusion Unit recommendations for reducing truancy (p 49);

- Social Exclusion Unit recommendations for reducing exclusions (p 53);

- encouragement of greater curricular flexibility at Key Stage 4, for example for young people in Education Action Zones (p 54);

- the priority set for Careers Service to focus on under-achieving, non-participating and disaffected young people (p 59);

- education attainment targets for young people in care (p 60);

- New Start projects for disaffected and disengaged young people (p 63);

- reforms to A levels and GNVQs and the development of lateral AS levels (p 76);

- widening participation partnerships in further education following the Kennedy report (p 92);

- plans for greater collaboration and strategic oversight of tertiary provision (p 91), including a role for Regional Development Agencies (p 94);

- plans for reform of college governing bodies and TEC boards to ensure greater accountability to local communities and more effective liaison with LEAs (p 92);

- 16 and 17 year olds to be entitled to day release or equivalent to study for an approved qualification (p 101).

Short- to medium-term recommendations

The second category of policies are those that we recommend within the context of the existing education and training system:

- uniform application of clear whole-school discipline policies based on positive reinforcement (p 44);

- greater pupil participation in decision-making, not just through school councils, but also through involving a wider range of pupils in a wider range of decisions including those affecting discipline (p 46);

- strong role for LEAs in reducing exclusions, for example through targeted work for particular groups at risk such as those disaffected at primary-secondary transfer, out-of-school provision for under-achievers, better co-ordination and collaboration across local services, and development of performance indicators) (p 51);

- special initiatives aimed at promoting participation and progression amongst young people in care (p 60);

- greater involvement of post-compulsory education institutions in the 14-16 age group (p 65);

- greater and more innovative use of initiatives to break down the boundaries between schools, the world of work, and the community (for example Associate Teachers, business units in schools, mentorship schemes, industry-specific and citizenship curriculum initiatives) (p 66);

- use of new information and communications technologies to develop 'virtual schools' not least to bring new entry and re-entry points to young people who are rarely present in school (p 67).

We argue in this book that the effectiveness of such initiatives is limited by broader factors outside of the control of local agencies.

The long-term policy agenda

The previous three chapters of this report have set out a wider and more long-term policy agenda in terms of the curriculum and qualifications structure for 14-19 year olds; the whole organisational framework of education, training and other services; and the funding of learning. The more extensive policies that we recommend need consideration are:

- The development of a unified 14-19 curriculum/qualifications framework, incorporating academic, general vocational and work-based qualifications. As we have argued, a unified curriculum and qualifications structure is vital to raising achievement for all and equipping young people with the broad knowledge, as well as the specialist skills, they need for the future (p 76).

- The integration of local services increasingly on the basis of a focus on the whole needs of client groups, rather than on the basis of professional and disciplinary boundaries. Such integration is particularly necessary for vulnerable young people and whilst this is recognised by policy-makers, reform remains a long-term, far-reaching and therefore complex prospect (p 85).

- Increased role for Regional Development Agencies in tertiary education and training, alongside the parallel development of beefed-up FEFC regional committees which involve stronger local authority representation, in order to develop greater coherence and co-ordination of provision (p 94).

- Regional government eventually to be the natural locus for light-touch planning and foresight of tertiary education and training (p 95).

● Development of a single allowance for 16-19 year olds to replace existing benefits and allowances, providing a coherent system of financial support for young people participating in education and training activity, along the lines of that introduced in Australia (p 99).

● Extension of traineeships across the full-time youth labour market to ensure that all young people entering jobs get training and develop marketable skills. The extension of the New Deal to the 16-18 age group could also be examined (p 101).

● The development of unified funding systems for post-16 education and training, organised on a regional basis. This would follow the initial development of a stronger regional capacity for tertiary education and training, as described above, but could act as a prelude to the eventual arrival of regional government. In the interim, we recommend the extension of the principles of the Further Education Funding Council methodology to all tertiary education and training (p 108).

Biblography

Armstrong D, Loudon R, McCready S, Wilson D, Istance D, Rees G (1997) *Status 0: a socio-economic study of young people on the margin.* NIERC

Aspire Consultants (1996) *Disaffection & non-participation in education, training and employment by individuals aged 18-20.* London: Department for Education and Employment

Association for Colleges *et al* (1994) *Post-compulsory education and training: a joint statement.* London: Association for Colleges

Audit Commission/OFSTED (1993) *Unfinished business: full-time educational courses for 16-19 year olds.* London: HMSO

Audit Commission (1996) *Misspent youth: young people and crime.* London: HMSO

Audit Commission (1998) *Changing partners.* London: Audit Commission

Barber M (1993) *Raising standards in deprived urban areas.* In National Commission on Education *Briefings.* London: Heinemann

Barber M and Brighouse T (1992) *Partners in change: enhancing the teaching profession.* London: Institute for Public Policy Research

Bates I and Riseborough G eds. (1993) *Youth and inequality.* Buckingham: Open University Press

Biehal *et al* (1995) *Moving On: Young people and leaving care schemes.* London: HMSO

Blackstone T (1998) *Qualifying for success: the response to the Qualifications and Curriculum Authority's Advice.* London: DfEE

Blyth E and Milner J eds. (1996) *Exclusions from school: inter-professional issues in policy and practice.* London: Routledge

Blunkett D (1996) *Colleges can help tackle disaffection – speech to Association of Colleges*, 21 November. London: Labour Party

Bynner J and Parsons S (1997) *It doesn't get any better: the impact of poor basic skills on the lives of 37 year olds.* London: The Basic Skills Agency

Carley M (1996) *Vocational education and positive progression routes: an overview of vocational education projects co-ordinated by Rathbone CI in the North West.* Manchester: Rathbone CI

Casey B and Smith D (1995) *Truancy and youth transitions.* Department for Education and Employment Youth Cohort Research Series Report No. 34. London: Policy Studies Institute

Chatrik B and Convery P (1998) 'News analysis' in *Working Brief*, May 1998

Cheng Y (1995) *Staying-on in full-time education after 16: do schools make a difference?* Department for Education and Employment Youth Cohort Research Series Report No.37, London: Policy Studies Institute

Children's Society (1997) *Tackling youth crime: response from The Children's Society*. London: The Children's Society

Cloward R and Ohlin L (1961) *Delinquency and opportunity*. London: Routledge and Kegan Paul

Cohen L, Manion L and Morrison K (1996) *A guide to teaching practice*. London: Routledge

Coles B (1995) *Youth and social policy: young citizenship and young careers*. London: UCL Press

Coles B (1996) *Youth transitions and youth policy: the need for co-ordination*. University of Warwick: Institute for Employment Research

Coles B, Rugg J and England J (1998, forthcoming) *Housing officers and multi-agency work with children and young people; on social housing estates*. London: Chartered Institute of Housing/Joseph Rowntree Foundation

Commission on Public Policy and British Business (1997) *Promoting Prosperity* London: IPPR/Vintage

Crequer N (1997) *A taste of work works wonders* London: Times Educational Supplement

Crime Concern (1992) *Family, school and community: towards a social crime prevention agenda*. Swindon: Crime Concern

Davis J (1990) *Youth and the condition of Britain: images of adolescent conflict*. London: Athlone Press

Dearing R (1996) *Review of qualifications for 16-19 year olds: full report*. London: SCAA

Department for Education (1992) *Exclusion: a discussion paper*. London: DfE

Department for Education and Employment (1995) *More willingly to school? An independent evaluation of the truancy and disaffected pupils GEST programme*. London: DfEE

Department for Education and Employment (1996) *Learning to compete: education and training for 14-19 year olds*. London: HMSO

Department for Education and Employment (1997a) *Permanent exclusions from schools in England 1995/6, 324/97*

Department for Education and Employment (1997b) *Youth cohort study: the activities and experiences of 16 year olds: England and Wales. 1996, 8/97*

Department for Education and Employment (1997c) *Participation in education and training by 16-18 year olds in England: 1986-1996, 159/97*

Department for Education and Employment (1997d) *Education and labour market status of young people aged 16-18 in England, 1990-96,* Statistical Bulletin 9/97

Department for Education and Employment (1997e) *Government-supported training: YT/MA/TfW England and Wales, 395/97*

Department for Education and Employment (1997f) *Qualifying for success.* London: HMSO

Department for Education and Employment (1997g) *Excellence in schools,* Cm 3681. London: HMSO

Department for Education and Employment (1998) *LEA Behaviour Support Plans.* Circular No. 1/98. London: DfEE

Department for Education and Employment (1998a) *Government-supported training: work-base training for young people and for adults – England and Wales.* Statistical Press Notice 270.98. London: DfEE

Department of Education and Science (1983) *Young people in the 80s: a survey.* London: HMSO

Department of Education and Science (1989) *Discipline in Schools* (The Elton Report). London: HMSO

Devlin A (1995) *Criminal classes: offenders at school.* Winchester: Waterside

Donovan N (ed.) (1998) *Second Chances: exclusion from school and equality of opportunity.* London: New Policy Institute

Education and Employment Select Committee (1998) *Disaffected Children.* London: The Stationery Office

Education and Employment Select Committee (1998a) *Further Education.* London: The Stationery Office

Ekinsmith C and Bynner J (1994) *The basic skills of young adults.* London: Basic Skills Agency

Evans K, Hodkinson P, Keep E, Maguire M, Raffe D, Rainbird H, Senker P and Unwin L (1997) *Working to learn (Issues in People Management, No. 18)*. London: Institute of Personnel and Development

Farreil P and Mittler H (1998) *Policy and practice in the assessment of pupils with special needs*. Manchester: Department of Education, University of Manchester and Rathbone C I

Finegold *et al* (1990) *A British Baccalaureate*. London: IPPR

Further Education Funding Council (1992) *Funding learning*. Coventry: Further Education Funding Council

Further Education Funding Council (1996) *Inclusive learning: report of the learning difficulties and/or disabilities committee*. Coventry: Further Education Funding Council

Garnett L (1992) *Leaving care and after*. London: National Children's Bureau

Godfrey R and Parsons C (1998) *Exclusion: the facts and figures*. London: Parliamentary Brief, Vol. 5, No. 5.

Graham J and Bowling B (1995) *Young people and crime: self-reported offending among 14-25 year olds in England and Wales*. Home Office Research Study 145, London: Home Office

Green A and Steedman H (1996) *Widening participation in further education and training: literature and issues survey*. London: Centre for Economic Performance

Green A and Steedman H (1997) *Into the twenty first century: an assessment of British skill profiles and prospects*. London: Centre for Economic Performance

Haggle A and Shaw C (1996) *Opportunity and disadvantage at age 16*. London: Policy Studies Institute

Hargreaves D (1994) *The mosaic of learning: schools and teachers for the next century*. London: Demos

Hayden C (1997) *Children excluded from primary school: debates, evidence and responses*. Buckingham: Open University Press

Hayden C (1997a) *Exclusion from primary school: children "in need" and children with "special educational need"* Emotional and Behavioural Difficulties, Vol.2 No 3 Winter 1997

Hayden C (1996) 'Primary school exclusions: the need for integrated solutions', in Blyth E and Milner J (eds.) *Exclusions from school: inter-professional issues in policy and practice*. London: Routledge

Highfield Junior School (1997) *Changing our school: promoting positive behaviour*. Plymouth: Highfield Junior School

Hodgson A and Spours K. eds. (1997) *Dearing and beyond: 14-19 qualifications, frameworks and systems*. London: Kogan Page

Hodkinson P, Sparkes A and Hodkinson H (1996) *Triumphs and fears: young people, markets and the transition from school to work*. London: David Fulton

Home Office (1988) *Behaviour and delinquency: a review of research*. London: HMSO

Hustler D, Callaghan J, Cockett M and McNeill J (1998) *Choices for life: an evaluation of Rathbone C*. Manchester Metropolitan University: Didsbury Educational Research Centre.

Illich I (1971) *Deschooling society*. New York: Calder and Boyers

Imich A (1994) *Exclusions from school: current trends and issues* Educational Research, vol.36, no 1, Spring 1994

Industrial Society (1997) *Speaking up, speaking out! 2020 Vision Programme Research Report*. London: Industrial Society

Istance D, Rees G and Williamson H (1994) *Young people not in education, training or employment in South Glamorgan*. S Glamorgan Training and Enterprise Council

Istance D and Williamson H (1996) *16 and 17 year olds in Mid-Glamorgan not in education, training or employment (Status 0)*. Mid Glamorgan Training and Enterprise Council

Jones G and Wallace C (1992) *Youth, family and citizenship*. Milton Keynes: Open University Press

Kennedy H (1997) *Learning works*. Coventry: Further Education Funding Council

Keys W and Fernandes C (1993) *What do students think about school? A report for the National Commission on Education*. Slough: National Foundation for Educational Research

Kinder K, Harland J, Wilkin A and Wakefield A (1996) *Three to remember: strategies for disaffected pupils*. Slough: National Foundation for Educational Research

Kinder K, Wakefield A and Wilkin A (1996a) *Talking back: pupil views on disaffection*. Slough: National Foundation for Educational Research

Kinder K and Wilkin A (1998) *With all respect: reviewing disaffection strategies*. Slough: National Foundation for Educational Research

Labour Party (1996) *Aiming higher: Labour's plans for reform of the 14-19+ curriculum.* London: Labour Party

Labour Party (1996b), *Lifelong Learning.* London: Labour Party

Labour Party (1997) *Boys will be boys?* London: Labour Party

Layard R, Robinson P and Steedman H (1995) *Lifelong Learning.* London: Centre for Economic Performance

Lewis E (1995) *Truancy: the partnership approach.* London: Home Office

McDonald R ed. (1997) *Youth, the 'underclass' and social exclusion.* London: Routledge

Maclagan I (1992) *A broken promise: the failure of youth training policy.* Youthaid/The Children's Society

Morgan D (1995) *Cities in schools: the bridge course, curriculum framework, mission statement.* Cambridge: Cities in Schools

Murray C (1990) *The emerging British underclass.* London: Institute of Economic Affairs

National Association for the Care and Resettlement of Offenders (1993) *Youth choices: improving the take-up of training by unemployed young people.* London: NACRO

National Commission on Education (1995) *Learning to Succeed After Sixteen,* London: National Commission on Education

National Commission on Education (1996) *Success against the odds: effective schools in disadvantaged areas.* London: Routledge

O'Keefe D (1994) *Truancy in English secondary schools: a report prepared for the DFE.* London: HMSO

OECD (1997) *Education at a Glance: OECD Indicators.* Paris: OECD

OFSTED (1993) *Education for disaffected pupils.* London: HMSO

OFSTED (1995) *A survey of careers education and guidance in schools.* London: HMSO

OFSTED (1995b) *Pupil referral units: the first twelve inspections.* London: HMSO

OFSTED (1995c) *Access, achievement and attendance in secondary schools.* London: HMSO

OFSTED/Social Services Inspectorate (1995) *The education of young people who are looked after.* London: HMSO

OFSTED (1996) *Exclusions from secondary schools 1995/6.* London: HMSO

Parsons C (1996) *Final report on the follow-up survey of permanent exclusions from schools in England 1995/6*. Canterbury: Christ Church College

Parsons C (1996a) *Exclusions from school: the public cost*. London: Commission on Racial Equality.

Parsons C/DfEE (1995) *National survey of local education authorities policies and procedures for the identification of and provision for, children who are out of school by reason of exclusion or otherwise*. London: Department for Education and Employment

Payne J (1995) *Options at 16 and outcomes at 24: A comparison of academic and vocational education and training routes*, Department for Education and Employment Youth Cohort Series Report No.35. London: Policy Studies Institute

Payne J (1995a) *Qualifications between 16-18: a comparison of achievements on routes beyond compulsory schooling*. Department for Education and Employment Youth Cohort Series Report No.32. London: Policy Studies Institute

Payne J (1995b) *Routes beyond compulsory schooling*. Department for Education and Employment Youth Cohort Series Report no 31. London: Policy Studies Institute

Qualifications and Curriculum Authority (1998) *Education for citizenship and the teaching of democracy in schools*. Advisory Group initial report. London: QCA

Raffe D (1993) *Participation of 16-18 year olds in education and training* in *National Commission on Education, Briefings*. London: Heinemann

Rathbone/CI, CSV, NACRO and TEN (1997) *Learning and earning: education, training and employment for all in the 21st century*. London: Rathbone CI, CSV, NACRO, TEN

Robinson P (1998) 'Education, Training and the Youth Labour Market' in Gregg, P and Wadsworth, J (eds.) *The State of Working Britain*. Centre for Economic Performance, London School of Economics

Rolfe H, Bryson A and Metcalf H (1996) *The effectiveness of TECs in achieving jobs and qualifications for disadvantaged groups*. London: Department for Education and Employment

Sammons P, Hillman J and Mortimore P (1995) *Key characteristics of effective schools*. London: Institute of Education/OFSTED

Sargant N and Tuckett A (1996) *The Learning Divide*. Leicester: NIACE

Scott P (1995) *A tertiary system.* Manchester: Society of Education Officers

Skilbeck M, Connell H, Lowe, N and Tait K (1994) *The vocational quest: new directions in education and training.* London: Routledge

Smith R (1998) *No lessons learnt: a survey of school exclusions.* London: The Children's Society

Social Exclusion Unit (1998) *Truancy and school exclusion.* London: The Stationery Office

Spours K (1995) *Post-compulsory education and training: statistical trends.* Learning for the Future Working Paper 7, London: Institute of Education/Centre for Education and Industry, University of Warwick.

Spours K and Lucas N (1996) *The formation of a national sector of incorporated colleges: beyond the FEFC model.* London: Institute of Education, National Association of Teachers in Further and Higher Education

Spours K and Young M (1996) *Dearing and Beyond: Steps and Stages to a Unified System.* British Journal of Education and Work, December

Stein M (1997) *What works in leaving care?* Ilford: Barnados.

Stephenson M (1996) *Cities in Schools: a new approach for excluded children and young people,* in Blyth E and Miller J (eds.) *Exclusion from school: policy and practice.* London: Routledge

Tomlinson S, ed. (1997) *Education 14-19: critical perspectives.* London: The Athlone Press

UNISON (1995) *Truancy: the neglected scandal.* London: UNISON

Unwin L (1995) *Staying the course: students' reasons for non-completion of full-time education courses in South and East Cheshire.* Middlewich: South and East Cheshire Education-Business Partnership

Wilkinson C (1995) *The drop out society: young people on the margin.* Youth Work Press

Williamson H (1995) *Policy responses to youth unemployment: cultures, careers and consequences for young people,* in *Jobs for Young Australians: an international conference (Adelaide)*

Williamson H (1996) *Young people on the edge: an individual or a social problem?* University of Warwick: Institute for Employment Research

Wragg T (1997) *Oh Boy.* London: Times Educational Supplement, 16 May

Endnotes

1.   Exclusion may be permanent or of fixed-term duration up to a period of 45 days in any one year. Schools may also exclude pupils unofficially or informally, as happens, for example, when parents agree voluntarily to withdraw a child and seek placement in another school, or when a pupil remains on school grounds but is prohibited from participating in activities with his or her peers.

2.   As originally drafted, the Government's Schools' Bill may have actually worsened the exclusion problem, since it excluded local authority representatives, who can act as a critical counterweight to the school governing body, from exclusion appeal panels. As a result of the Social Exclusion Unit's report, the legislation has been amended.

3.   Interestingly the 1995 British Household Panel Survey showed female 10-15 year olds were twice as likely to have low levels of self-esteem than their male counterparts and also reported significantly higher rates of being 'worried a lot' about being bullied.

4.   The Audit Commission figures should now be treated with caution, as the fieldwork was conducted in 1991/2. It was influential upon the design of the Further Education Funding Council's methodology for funding colleges, which seeks to reward student retention and achievement.

5.   This figure cannot be compared with success rates in the further education sector since FEFC definitions of retention and achievement do not take account of drop-out in the few weeks at the beginning and end of each year.

6.   'Status Zero' was coined in fieldwork for the analysis of those not participating in education, training or employment in Mid-Glamorgan. Howard Williamson notes that 'Status Zer0' [sic] has proved to be a contentious term ... during the fieldwork, 'status 0' was simply a technical concept to depict the status of those young people not in education, training or employment ... it was felt, however, that 'Status Zer0' represented a powerful metaphor for young people who appeared to count for nothing and be going nowhere. This terminology, however, created a political furore at the local level and references to 'status 0' in the research report were replaced by 'status A' (Williamson in MacDonald ed. 1997: 82).

7.   The Department for Education and Employment has recently conducted a consultation exercise on the creation of a single database

of the education and training participation and achievements of young people aged 14-21. It is intended to include a single longitudinal record for each young person in England, with a few exceptions, constructed by linking together records from various datasets.

8. Adequate statistics might require an individual pupil identifier from age 14 and preferably earlier (National Insurance numbers are currently issued at age 15).

9. Those in employment without training are very similar in profile to those in government-supported training, but are less well qualified than those in work who get training.

10. The government has also made available £2 million from the Standards Fund for work-related learning projects for 14-16 year olds. These are focused particularly on socially disadvantaged and under-achieving young people.

11. Until the School Standards and Framework Bill takes effect grant-maintained schools will continue to exist, with their sixth forms funded in a similar manner by the Funding Agency for Schools.